PRAISE FOR SOME OF ROSEMARY ELLEN GUILEY'S PREVIOUS INSPIRING WORKS

THE MIRACLE OF PRAYER

"Prayer heals. . . . *The Miracle of Prayer* honors our rediscovery of this ancient realization. Anyone facing illness or other problems will be inspired by Rosemary Guiley's magnificent account. There's no hype in these pages, and Guiley isn't selling any particular religion. She honors the majesty, the power, and the mystery of prayer in an evenhanded, admirable way. This is a wonderful book, straight from the heart."

—Larry Dossey, M.D., author of
Healing Words and *Recovering the Soul*

ANGELS OF MERCY

"So impressive I bought a half-dozen copies to give away to friends."
—Rev. Grace B. Bradley, *Sparrow Hawk Villager* (OK)

TALES OF REINCARNATION

"Filled with information. . . . As an introduction and overview, this book is excellent."

—*FATE* magazine (St. Paul)

BOOKS BY ROSEMARY ELLEN GUILEY

The Miracle of Prayer
Blessings: Prayers for the Home and Family
Wellness: Prayers for Comfort and Healing
Angels of Mercy
I Bring You Glad Tidings

I Bring You
GLAD TIDINGS

Inspiring True Stories of Christmas Angels

Written and Compiled by
Rosemary Ellen Guiley

POCKET BOOKS
New York   London   Toronto   Sydney   Singapore

POCKET BOOKS, a division of Simon & Schuster Inc.
1230 Avenue of the Americas, New York, NY 10020

Library of Congress Cataloging-in-Publication Data

Guiley, Rosemary.
    I bring you glad tidings / Rosemary Ellen Guiley.
        p. cm.
    ISBN 978-1-4516-0604-1
    1. Angels—Miscellanea.   I. Title.
  BL477.G88 1999
  291.2'15—dc21   99-046771

First Pocket Books hardcover printing December 1999

10 9 8 7 6 5 4 3 2 1

Cover illustration by Lina Levy
Cover photo courtesy of Art Resource

Designed by Celia Fuller and Laura Lindgren

Printed in the U.S.A.

For Joann Matias

Contents

Acknowledgments   ix

Introduction   1

The Sleeping Angel   9

Nana's Song   29

Mirror of Truth   37

I Will Be Your Rock   49

Lost and Found   61

Keep Your Intention on God   69

A Heavenly Doctor Makes a House Call   79

The Christmas Wish   85

Peace, Be Still   99

The Miracle of the Light and the Life   105

The Angelic Mechanic   129

The Christmas Visit   139

Choices and Consequences   149

A Brush of Angel Wings   155

The Heart-Shaped Stone   165

An Angel and a Spare   177

A Christmas Gift from an
"Angel Animal" Cat   185

The Greatest Gift   193

Resources   205

Acknowledgments

Whenever I undertake a book of personal stories, I never know who will be my sources and where I will find them. But I do trust that the angelic forces will guide me to the right people. And so they did for this book.

I would especially like to thank Norm Braverman, the creator of Angelhaven.com, the biggest and best site on the Internet for angels. Norm was my main angel on earth. Through Angelhaven.com, I connected with some of the wonderful people featured in these pages. Getting to know Norm led to my joining Angelhaven.com as a regular columnist and contributor. Read more about Angelhaven.com in the back of this book in "Resources."

I also received help from two other angels on earth, Rev. Jayne Howard and Mary Dansicker, who introduced me to contributors to this book.

Jayne, author of *Commune with the Angels,* is renowned for her inspirational and motivational work in partnership with the angels. Mary Dansicker is owner and operator of Joshua's Lighthouse Angels, a wonderful gift store in Reisterstown, Maryland. Mary, who lost her young son, Joshua, helps the bereaved.

My deep appreciation and thanks go to the following persons who shared their stories:

Bea Sheftel, for "The Christmas Wish." Bea dedicates her story to her mother, Frances, and her father, Sal.

Jean Haines Reistle for "A Brush of Angel Wings."

Kelly K. for "Mirror of Truth."

Janie M. for "Choices and Consequences."

Juliet H. for "Peace, Be Still."

Christina Gautreaux for "Nana's Song."

Terri and David Levy and Yvonne Warner for "The Sleeping Angel."

Linda and Allen Anderson for "A Christmas Gift from an 'Angel Animal' Cat," adapted from the story by the same title, copyright Allen and Linda Anderson, published in *Angel Animals® Newsletter,* fall 1998. Used with permission. See the "Resources" section for more information about the Andersons' work.

Rev. Toni G. Boehm for "Keep Your Intention on God."

Patricia, Joe Sr., and Joe Jr. Almazan for "The Greatest Gift."

Vondalyn Reddick for "A Heavenly Doctor Makes a House Call."

Gary and Linda Woodward for "The Miracle of the Light and the Life."

Charlotte Abell for "The Heart-Shaped Stone."

Dawn Eslinger for "I Will Be Your Rock."

Jackie O'Brien for "The Christmas Visit."

Mardell B. for "An Angel and a Spare."

Jason and Rick (pseudonyms) for "Lost and Found" and "The Angelic Mechanic," respectively.

Everyone shared their stories from deep within their hearts. I know their stories will touch your heart, too.

I Bring You
GLAD TIDINGS

Introduction

Christmas celebrates the birth of Jesus Christ, and the story of Jesus cannot be told without angels. The messengers of God play a prominent role, from the conception of Jesus to his death and resurrection. The archangel Gabriel announces to Mary that she has been chosen to be the vessel for the Christ. When the infant Jesus is born, angels appear in the heavens and tell shepherds, "Be not afraid, for behold, I bring you glad tidings of a great joy which will come to all the people." Angels watch over and protect the family, guiding them to safety in Egypt and then back to their homeland. Angels are with Jesus in his ministry. They stand at his empty tomb and confirm his resurrection.

At Christmastime, we honor the life and ministry of Jesus and the Christ consciousness within the human soul. It is a time for glad tidings, for rejoicing, for love, and for renewal. We are reminded that whatever trials we face in life, we have the strength to meet those trials and prevail.

Our thoughts naturally turn to angels at Christmastime, when songs and art celebrate them. Though angels are with us all the time, regardless of season, our encounters with them at this time of year take on special meaning and poignancy.

Angels are real beings of awesome power and mystery. They are God's messengers, whose role is to keep us attuned to the heart of God. Through this attunement, unconditional love flows freely, and we are protected, comforted, guided, and redeemed.

While not human, angels are nonetheless part of us, for all things in this great and glorious universe are interconnected. We realize the angelic link, the angelic part of ourselves, through our heart and through the Higher Self. The heart hears and knows Truth. The heart gives love and receives love. The Higher Self receives the guidance that comes from the Divine in intuition, dreams, meditation, prayer, and synchronicity. The Higher Self has vision that builds faith.

An encounter with an angel is called an angelophany. It seldom involves great winged and radiant beings. Rather, angels meet us on our own levels of acceptable perception. They may manifest as a visual impression, or an inner voice, or an external voice. They may be someone who appears to be human. They may be an invisible presence or force; or a message in a dream, as in Janie's story in this book, "Choices and Consequences." Angels also influence us through the words and actions of others. "The Greatest Gift," about the Almazan family, testifies to an experience of this type. And angels speak to us through nature and through animals, as exemplified in Linda and Allen Anderson's winsome story, "A Christmas Gift from an 'Angel Animal' Cat."

My own interaction with angels has been in these various ways. My awareness of angels was initiated some years ago in my dreams, in which I was guided and given spiritual instruction by a glowing being I could only call an angel. These dreams eventually came to an end—such experiences serve as a wake-up call—but opened me to the presence of the angelic realm. The more I "allowed" the idea of angels, the more aware of them I became, both on the inner plane and in the exterior world. Not only was I blessed with experiences of angels concerned in the affairs of the human realm, I also sensed and saw the glorious angelic presence that animates the world of nature.

One Christmas I was very much alone—far away from family and friends, and no one to call special in my life. The holidays are hard on you when you are alone. In an effort to find some holiday cheer, I put up a Christmas tree. Though it sparkled quite prettily, I still felt little cheer. One morning I awoke and went downstairs, and was astonished to find the Christmas tree all lit up. In the moment of my astonishment, a voice as clear as a bell said to me, "You are not alone." I was flooded with a tremendous warmth. The lights went off. I stood for a moment stunned. I had, as usual, unplugged the lights before retiring. I thought that perhaps I'd forgotten to unplug them, and that something was wrong with the wiring. On checking the plug, I saw that it was indeed out of the socket.

Had I imagined the flash of lights? The voice? I could not convince myself that I had. My heart told me otherwise. I had been given an angelic sign that I had no need to despair, that I was indeed not alone, and in fact was never alone. My present "aloneness" was a matter of perspective—a perspective that I had the power to change. My spirits were lifted considerably, and I enjoyed the remainder of the holiday season in an optimistic frame of mind. I even cherished my solitude as a special time for contemplation. It was an important turning point in emotional healing.

The experience of the external voice is not uncommon in exceptional experiences, and is well documented in the literature of mysticism. It is called audition: a clear and powerful voice that comes from beyond one's own self. Throughout the ages, men and women have heard through audition the voice of God and angels, usually in experiences that bring illumination and transformation.

Angels seem to have a fondness for getting our attention through light. This is not surprising, since they are beings of light who ride the brilliant emanations from the Source of All Being. Some wonderful examples of light are in this volume: in "The Miracle of the Light and the Life," the poignant story of Gary and Linda Woodward and their son, Chris, and in "Peace, Be Still," Juliet's story of comfort and healing.

Another intriguing way that angels interact with us is the "mysterious stranger" encounter. They occur when a person is in a dilemma and needs quick action. A mysterious person suddenly appears out of nowhere and provides a solution. Mysterious strangers can be male or female of any race. Most often, they are male—usually a fresh-looking, clean-cut youth. They are invariably well-dressed, polite, and knowledgeable about the crisis at hand. They often are calm, but can be forceful, and they know just what to do.

They speak, though sparingly. They are convincingly real as flesh-and-blood humans. However, once the problem has been solved, the mysterious strangers vanish. It is their abrupt and strange disappearance that makes people question whether they have been aided by mortals or angels. In this volume, "Lost and Found" and "The Angelic Mechanic" are examples of mysterious stranger angels.

Given their subtle and sometimes disguised methods, how do you know for certain when you've been in contact with an angel? I am asked that question often by both believers in angels and skeptics alike. The answer is surprisingly simple: no other explanation will satisfy, no matter how hard you try to find one. Our contact with the Divine comes through the heart and the soul, not through the mind. The mind wants—even demands—rational, logical thought. It wants proof, statistics, and quantifiable, tangible things. The world of science was born of mind. The heart and the soul seek Truth. Truth is intangible. It cannot be held, measured, or defined. Rather, it is known. To find Truth, we are led into the mystery of God. When we have touched the mystery, the heart knows.

Those who enter onto the spiritual path through devotion, prayer, meditation, contemplation, study, and good works learn to trust the heart. An inner knowing arises. Truth is perceived and experienced, and no doubts cast by any skeptic can turn aside our vision.

I am also often asked if it is possible for people to become angels after death. The answer to that question is that they become like angels. All things are woven together in the wholeness of creation. The spark of God, the spark of the angelic realm, resides within each and every soul. It waits to be nourished, to grow, and to blossom in life. After death, when the soul is freed of physical limitations, it can express itself in many new ways, including angel-like functions. As several stories here attest, people who have lost loved ones have felt their loved ones take on the role of protective or guardian angel.

All sorts of angelophanies are described in the stories in this book, demonstrating that there are many ways to experience the grace of angels and receive a revelation from their glad tidings. For some people, the experience has drama; for others, the experience is as subtle and soft as the whispers of a breeze. But all experiences share one thing in common: transformation. For no matter how we are graced by the angelic realm, we are profoundly changed in heart, mind, and soul.

Yvonne Warner, who is featured in "The Sleeping Angel," describes a miracle as "the expression of love from God." Each and every one of these stories demonstrates a miracle. There is no such distinction as a small miracle or a big miracle. All miracles, all expressions of the love of God, are great, whether they be a rescue from danger, a healing of catastrophic illness, a turning point in sorrow, or the joy of family love.

Behind every trial described in this book is a triumph. Each story shows in its own unique way a triumph of the human spirit to overcome all adversity and to become lit with an inner fire that is the love of God.

The
Sleeping
Angel

Every day, our paths cross with the paths of strangers. Some meetings are fleeting. Some are of momentous significance, great turning points of mind and heart. A seemingly chance encounter is not an accident or coincidence at all, but a purposeful weaving of God's tapestry of souls. Angels play a role in this weaving of destinies. They give us a nudge here, a prompt there. One Christmas in upstate New York, angels brought strangers together, and lives were changed.

Yvonne Warner never expected, nor intended, to become the "Angel Lady." Yet she was gifted with otherworldly sight from birth, and from infancy was aware of great spiritual beings she came to call angels and masters. As she grew older, she communicated with them, was visited by them, and traveled into wondrous realms with them. As a trance channel, she received messages from the dead, which were of great comfort to the living.

She understood these gifts of hers to be gifts of the Spirit, as described in the Bible.

Young Yvonne's sense of destiny was that she would be guided in what she should do in life, and that everything was to be done out of love. "I work with and for the Father," she said. She believed in miracles. "A miracle is the expression of love from God," she told others. "It is up to us to make miracles happen every day by expressing that love."

Life handed Yvonne a full plate. By the time she was in her mid-thirties, she had been married twice, a mother, rich, poor, and briefly homeless. All of her work had been to protect or help and heal others. She had worked as a police officer and an undercover officer. She had been an acupuncturist, a primary caregiver for AIDS patients, an HIV counselor, a substance abuse counselor, a children's education counselor, an art therapist, and a caregiver to the dying. People had died in her arms and been healed in her arms. Yvonne always felt humble that she could be of help to others. "Whatever I have to give you has been given by the Father and the Father within," she would say.

She received daily counsel from the angels. They told her never to worry, that her needs would always be met. She followed their guidance, not always knowing where it would lead, but having complete faith and trust that it would always be right and true. She learned that her purpose concerned uplifting her brothers and sisters of humanity to know and understand that God does always watch over them, and is always available. She learned that in return for giving, her own cup was always filled.

When Yvonne was thirty-six, two benign tumors were discovered on her coccyx at the end of her spine. She was between jobs—she had lost one when a counseling center closed, and found another, but had not yet started it. Two surgeries to remove the tumors left Yvonne in excruciating pain and temporarily unable to walk. She had to give up the new job. She lay in bed wondering how she was going to survive—how she was going to put food on the table and pay the bills.

One day as she slept in bed an angel visited her in her dreams. "You are going to make angels," the great being said.

Yvonne awakened perplexed as to how these instructions would be executed. The angel had not told her how to go about it, but simply to do it. Yvonne knew that she, like every human being, had to find her own way. Guidance is given, but if we are told precisely what to do, then we do not grow. We do not learn. It is our experience that refreshes the soul and advances our wisdom.

Yvonne had purchased some exquisite ceramic angels. She felt uplifted every time she looked at them. They reminded her that there was a presence greater than she that was with her all the time. As the Bible indicated, every time someone needed guidance or an answer, God sent an angel. And God's angels looked in on her often. Yvonne thought everyone should have an angel figurine to remind them of the divine presence around them, to lift them in the same way, and to act as a messenger from God.

An "awesome unfolding" was the only way Yvonne could describe how events led her to make angels. At the end of her street lived a woman who had a ceramics shop. Yvonne could barely walk, but immediately upon awakening from her dream, she felt compelled to hobble down the street and seek out this woman's advice. The shop was closed, but a sign said it would open at 7 P.M. She hobbled home. At 7 P.M. she returned to the shop, but it was still closed. Noting the phone number on the door, she thought she would call and leave a message. Spying a pay phone, she placed the call but somehow dialed a wrong number. Frustrated, tired, and in pain, Yvonne decided to put the whole thing off. Then she heard a voice whisper to her, "Turn around." She turned and saw lights on in the shop.

In great pain, Yvonne limped back and went through the door. Inside she met the proprietor, who was getting ready to teach a class in making ceramics. The students were assembled. "I want to make angels," Yvonne announced. "Can you show me how?"

"I can show you," said the woman, "but you can't join the class— it's full."

"You don't understand," said Yvonne. "I'm supposed to be here."

"I'm sorry," the proprietor said gently. "I don't have enough room."

Just then a woman dashed into the shop. She had to drop out of the class, she said, with profuse apologies.

The students and proprietor all looked at Yvonne in astonishment. "You see," Yvonne said, "I *am* supposed to be here!"

Yvonne joined the class and learned how to work with ceramics. She made one angel. One person saw it, loved it, and told others. From her bedside, Yvonne was suddenly in business as the "Angel Lady."

She recovered from her surgeries and devoted herself to making her porcelain beauties. They sold wherever she took them. She went to flea markets, galleries, crafts shows, and malls. She named her business Yvonne's Miracles. She made angels and cherubs by the thousands, each one by hand every step of the way. Each was unique in its decorations. Some were glazed for outdoor use. The heavenly angels guided her hands. "Never worry," the angels said. "Just make the angels for us. Each one is for someone. You will not know who they are for." True to her guidance, every angel Yvonne made found its way to the person for whom it was meant. She could feel it when an angel changed hands. She sold many and gave many away. Her sales enabled her to support herself. The angels, she said, fed her.

At Christmastime, Yvonne rented table space in the shopping mall in Middletown, New York. Business from holiday shoppers was good, so when Christmas neared the following year, Yvonne rented table space again. She hired a woman, Florence, to help her sell her creations.

One morning, as Yvonne prepared to go to the mall to work, she heard the angels tell her that someone would be coming by who had lost a loved one. This person would purchase an angel for the gravesite. Yvonne was to give that person a certain poem, because the family member who had passed away wanted to let the family know that he or she was all right, and the passing was supposed to happen. Those left behind should be happy, because their loved one was no longer in pain and suffering.

The poem was of anonymous authorship, found and given to Yvonne by a friend. Yvonne had it written on a piece of paper. She located it, put it in a box, and took it to the mall. She told Florence, "Somebody is going to come by who has lost someone. They are to receive this poem along with the angel."

The strands of Yvonne's destiny were about to be interwoven with the lives of Terri and David Levy and members of their families.

.   .   .

For six years, Terri's older sister, Mary, had battled breast cancer, determined to survive. She had three children; she wanted more than anything to live for them. She endured many ups and downs during the course of her illness. Things would look hopeful, and then not so hopeful. Whenever she felt particularly low, she called Terri, who lived about three-and-a-half hours away by car. "I'm going to live, right?" she would ask. "I'm going to make it, aren't I?" Terri always said the right words of hope to bring Mary's spirits back up.

But determination and words of hope did not prevail. The end, when it came at last, came quickly.

For about two weeks, Terri had missed connecting with Mary by phone. Then a call came one April morning: Make haste to the hospital, for Mary is dying and not expected to last the night.

Terri rushed to the hospital. Mary was already semicomatose, unable to talk to those she loved. She could only move her head a little and moan, and she moaned in response to what others said.

Terri was crushed by agonizing guilt. If only she had been able to talk to Mary earlier, perhaps she could have helped her hold on. But in the same grief-stricken moment, she realized that perhaps Mary had known that the time for talk was over, that it was time for her to go.

Terri assured Mary that it was okay for her to go, and that her children would be well taken care of. She asked Mary if she could understand. Mary moaned. Terri felt deep in her heart that Mary could hear her, could understand. She searched for recognition in Mary's unseeing, half-closed eyes. For a long time there was no reaction—and then came an obvious wink at Terri. "She winked at me!" Terri exclaimed, delighted.

She asked Mary if she could see any of the members of the family who were deceased. Mary moaned. But shortly, she suddenly rose up and reached toward the window of her room, as though she saw something others could not.

Terri did not spend the night at the hospital, but left Mary in the company of her husband and a friend. Later in the evening, she heard a song on the radio, "I've Been Talking to My Angel." Mary was keenly interested in angels, had them all over her house. Her interest inspired Terri to read about angels and collect them. Now Terri had an odd feeling that the song on the radio was Mary's way of talking to her, telling her not to cry, that she was going to a better place. Terri wondered if the song marked Mary's passing.

The song marked the opening of the gates of the Great Mystery of Death. The next morning, twelve hours later, Mary died. She was forty-two.

In the weeks following her death, Mary's presence was apparent to Terri and other members of the family. Her younger sister, Johnita, was awakened by Mary's voice calling her name and talking to her. Mary pledged to help the family. Terri occasionally heard soft, beautiful music—angel music. For both Terri and Johnita, there were physical sensations—feelings of being touched, of shivers and tingling. Their experiences were puzzling to Terri's husband, David, who believed in an afterlife but not necessarily communication between the living and the dead, and who had no marked interest in angels.

Terri struggled with her grief and with the guilt that lingered over the fact that she never had a final conversation with Mary. The weeks passed into months.

Soon the holiday season had arrived: the first Christmas without Mary.

On the Sunday before Christmas, David scurried around trying to get his last-minute chores and shopping done. He zipped to the Middletown mall. As he hurried down the aisles, his eye was caught by a table set up in the middle zone, though he couldn't see what was on the table. Part of him knew he had to press on, as there were still many things to be done, but another part of him felt strangely compelled to go and look at the table.

As he got closer, his body started to tingle. The closer he got, the more the tingling spread throughout his entire body. He had no idea why, and he still couldn't see what was on the table.

When he finally reached the front of the table, his whole body was tingling, especially his head. He gazed down on porcelain statues of angels and cherubs in various sizes and poses. They were beautiful, and each one was different. Though David believed in angels, he wasn't particularly drawn to them. Now he felt an inner command to examine each and every statue carefully. It was the most bizarre sensation, but David was unable to let skepticism take over. He simply went with the flow. He held some of them and turned them to look at all their sides and angles.

After inspecting most of the display, he suddenly "felt" Mary say to him, *Get me this one.* He picked up an angel and literally started to shake. He knew this was the one Mary wanted. It was a sleeping angel with a pretty pink bow. He knew he had to buy it for her grave—that this was what Mary wanted.

This impulse would not normally have occurred to David, for it ran counter to his Jewish upbringing. According to Jewish tradition, flowers and other adornments are considered distracting at a gravesite. If anything is placed at a grave, it is a simple rock, which serves as a physical remembrance that the grave has been visited. Terri's family was Catholic, but even his exposure to Catholic customs would not have prompted a spontaneous thought to purchase an angel for Mary's grave. Yet David had no doubt that he was being guided to do so.

Watching David, Yvonne intuitively was drawn to him, yet had no idea that he was the one for whom the poem was meant. It was almost time to close, and it was Yvonne's last day at the mall. No one had claimed the poem.

David gave his choice to Yvonne for purchase. She was warm and friendly. She explained to him that she was the maker of the statues. "Each one is different because an actual angel guides my hands as I make them," she explained with a smile. Yvonne added that she usually worked out of her house, but for the holidays she came to the mall. In one hour she was closing down and would not return to the mall until next year. David was one of her last customers.

David asked if the angel could be placed outdoors. When Yvonne replied yes, he told her about Mary, and that he would be placing the sleeping angel by her grave.

Yvonne felt a shiver of electricity race through her. Tears spilled from her eyes. *How profound, how sweet,* she thought. *He's the one.*

"I have been waiting for you," she said. Startled, David gave her a quizzical look. "An angel told me someone would come and purchase an angel for a grave. When that person came, I should give them this poem." She produced a piece of paper and handed it to David.

David read:

When tomorrow starts without me, and I'm not there to see;
If the sun should rise and find your eyes all filled with tears for me;
I wish so much you wouldn't cry the way you did today,

while thinking the many things we didn't get to say.

I know how much you love me, as much as I love you,

and each time you think of me, please try to understand,

that an Angel came and called my name and took me by the hand,

and said my place was ready in heaven far above,

and that I'd have to leave behind all those I dearly love.

But as I turned to walk away, a tear fell from my eye,

for all life, I'd always thought I didn't want to die.

I had so much to live for and so much yet to do,

it seemed almost impossible that I was leaving you.

I thought of all the yesterdays, the good ones and the bad,

I thought of all the love we shared and all the fun we had.

If I could relive yesterday, I thought, just for a while,

I'd say good-bye and kiss you and maybe see you smile.

But then I fully realized that this could never be,

for emptiness and memories would take the place for me.

And when I thought of worldly things that I'd miss come tomorrow,

I thought of you, and when I did, my heart was filled with sorrow.

But when I walked through heaven's gates I felt so much at home.

When God looked down and smiled at me, from his great golden throne,
he said, "This is eternity and all I've promised you."
Today for life on earth is past but here it starts anew.
I promise no tomorrow, but today will always last
and since each day's the same day, there's no longing for the past.
But you have been forgiven and now at last you're free.
So won't you take my hand and share my life with me?
So when tomorrow starts without me, don't think we're apart,
for every time you think of me, I'm right here in your heart.

The poem was signed "Author unknown."

David placed the poem with the angel in the little shopping bag given him by Yvonne and thanked her.

On Christmas Day, Terri's family gathered at the home of her mother. David approached Terri and Johnita, and asked if he could speak to them alone. Bewildered, they agreed and went into an upstairs bedroom where they had privacy.

David offered the shopping bag and a letter written by him. Terri and Johnita read the letter. It began, "While I do believe in the hereafter and I do believe our loved ones look down upon us and smile, I had not believed that those who have passed on could communicate so easily with us, as you have claimed to be communicating with your sister Mary. But I write this to tell you that my views have changed. Because she recently touched me." The letter went on to describe David's trip to the shopping mall and his discovery of the angel statues, and the amazing message from Yvonne.

As Terri and Johnita read, their vision blurred with tears. It was so incredible—and even more incredible that it had happened to David.

They were so overcome by the story that they forgot about the gift inside the shopping bag, until David reminded them to open it. There sat the precious sleeping angel with the pink bow. Terri and Johnita cried and laughed. Why, the angel's feet looked just like Mary's feet! They were dumbfounded when they turned the angel over and saw a date inscribed on the bottom. The day and month were the same as David's birthday. And the day, month, and year marked a month's anniversary for Mary's death. The "coincidences" were too incredible to be true.

They reread the letter and poem many times, soaking up every nuance. One thing was clear—they knew they had to speak to Yvonne, the "Angel Lady."

They called Yvonne after Christmas. It took some courage—what would they say to her? Would she even talk to them? But when they finally did call, they were greeted by a warm and friendly voice. Yvonne made them feel instantly comfortable. Terri, Johnita, and Mary's sixteen-year-old daughter, Corrie, joined in the conversation. Yvonne explained, "Mary wanted you to have that poem to help you heal and be happy again. To help you to get on with your lives." It was just what they needed to hear.

Yvonne gave them other messages from Mary, talking to them for over an hour, every word infusing them with comfort. They peppered her with questions. What were angels like? How did she experience them? How did she know to put that date on the bottom of the sleeping angel? Yvonne said she could not explain the date—she simply decorated her angels according to her guidance. Yvonne answered all their questions and confirmed many of the signs they felt they'd had from Mary. Yvonne wanted them to understand that there is a realm much higher and brighter after death, and that those who no longer have physical form do not want their loved ones to be sad and depressed, but joyful. At one point, Yvonne said, "What I'm getting doesn't make sense to me, but I'm hearing that you should relax and have some chocolate." Terri and Johnita laughed. Mary had always been a "chocoholic."

Mary became like a guardian angel to her family, and her presence brought the family even closer together. Yvonne became a close friend, part of the family. For Terri and Johnita, Mary awakened the "sleeping angel" within, and now they were on a glorious spiritual journey of discovery, their path illuminated by their angels, those in heaven and those on earth.

Nana's Song

On Christmas Eve, Christina Gautreaux's family gathered in the home of her grandmother Nana in Los Altos, California. It was a tiny house, but the family deemed it was best to celebrate the holiday there, rather than risk moving Nana around on a winter night.

A stroke had felled Nana—whose given name was Anne—some two years earlier, when she was seventy-eight. Aunt Jeanne had found her in a helpless state in her bathroom. The stroke exacted a cruel toll upon the little woman, the proud matriarch of an Italian family, whose parents had immigrated to America from the old country. Nana was left nearly totally paralyzed, and worst of all, she was rendered speechless. Efforts with speech therapy proved futile. Nana struggled valiantly to say just the names of her family, but even that was impossible.

For more than two years, the only sound Nana could make was "na na na na na na," like her nickname. It could mean anything. If she needed something, she said, "Na na na na na." If someone made her laugh: "Na na na na na." If she was angry: "Na na na na na." Nana communicated in response to questions by using feeble facial expressions, nodding or shaking her head, and putting different tones of voice into the one syllable she could utter.

Widowed years earlier, Nana lived in her little house. After the stroke, she stayed on, aided by a helper and family members. The close-knit family did the best they could to make Nana comfortable. While awake, she was confined to a chair or a wheelchair. The garden that had flourished under her green thumb could only be gazed upon. She listened to music—there was an old-fashioned reginaphone that played metal records—and she watched television. Woe be unto the unfortunate soul who interfered with her favorite program, *Lawrence Welk.* Nana would give them a tongue-lashing.

And so on this Christmas Eve, the family was piled into her house. Besides Christina, who was four years old, there were her mother, Pat; her father, Bill; her sisters, Gigi and Cheryl; her brother Mike; and Aunt Jeanne and her daughter Lisa. The family enjoyed a hearty meal. Afterward, the children plunged into a happy frenzy of opening presents. When all the gifts had been exchanged, and all the oohing and aahing had subsided, the children played with their new toys and the adults relaxed and shared stories. Nana, mute, listened and watched.

Suddenly, to everyone's surprise, Nana opened her mouth and began to sing. In a shaky, wavering and faint voice that everyone had thought was lost forever, she slowly and carefully sang her favorite Christmas carol, "Silent Night."

The room fell silent as the entire family sat spellbound. Mouths were open in astonishment. Pat and Jeanne, Nana's daughters, burst into tears. Even at the tender age of four, Christina knew something amazing was happening. She felt the room fill with emotions.

Nana sang most of the first verse to the song and then rested, quiet. Pat leaped from her chair and rushed to hug and kiss her precious mother. "How? How?" she kept crying. Nana simply nodded, as though her singing were the most normal of events. As the family erupted in joy and amazement, she radiated great happiness.

Everyone knew they had witnessed a miracle—a miracle brought by the angels. Hark, the herald angels sing at Christmas, and the angels had given the gift of voice back to Nana for one short, shining moment. But oh, what a moment!

The words to "Silent Night" were the last words that Nana ever spoke. Four years later, her little body riddled with cancer, Nana passed into her own silent and holy night.

For Christina, the Christmas miracle was emblazoned upon her memory in vivid detail. She could not hear "Silent Night" without feeling the power of miracles flow through her. Years later, long after Nana was gone and Christina was grown, she had an angel experience that reconnected her to that strange and wondrous night in a different way.

Christina's interest in angels led her to books and stories, where she read about other people's encounters with their guardian angels. Wistfully, she wondered when she would meet hers. One evening before drifting off to sleep, she prayed to God to send her angel to her that night.

She had this dream:

I walked into a room of angels. There were about eight of them. They appeared to take on a human form (no wings), but I knew they were angels. Most were women. There was one who apparently was the "head" angel. I sat

down on a couch, and one by one, they came up to me, and each of them gave me a big hug. We would share kind words, though I remember only one thing that was said. The last angel I hugged and spoke with looked to the head angel and said, "She's a lot like us." The head angel replied, "Of course she is."

I will never, ever forget the next thing that happened. I was looking straight ahead and suddenly felt as if someone were sitting to my left. I hadn't felt a movement, nor did I feel pressure. I just turned my head, and right next to me was "my" angel. She had curly blond hair and charcoal blue eyes. Rosy red chubby cheeks and a beautiful smile. Her smile warmed my heart, and the only thing I said to her was that she had "the most beautiful eyes."

Christina awoke and knew immediately that at last she had met her own angel. She called her "Cara" without knowing why. The angel had never given her name. It had come spontaneously to Christina as she lay still in bed after awakening, reveling in the dream. She saw the name against her closed eyes.

Then one day Christina came home from work and found a beautiful porcelain angel on her kitchen table. It was weathered and old, like an antique. Beside it was a note from her mother, who had stopped by and left the angel. It had belonged to Nana.

Christina remembered where it had hung in Nana's house, near the dining room table. As she gazed at the angel, she realized with a start that it looked exactly like Cara in her dream.

"Cara" means "dear" in Italian. From the depths of heaven, Nana had reached out through the angels to send a greeting of love.

To this very day, Christina cannot listen to "Silent Night" without breaking down and crying. The song speaks to her of hope, amazement, and restored faith in everything miraculous and spiritual. It speaks to the inner strength that every person carries within their soul, strength to do the impossible, even if only for a moment.

Christina prays that someday she will sing "Silent Night" when she is as old and beautiful as Nana was, the night the angels came.

Mirror
of Truth

The last time Kelly saw her father was the day he asked her if she and her little brother wanted to come and have dinner with him. Her brother wanted to go, but Kelly said no. She'd been invited to spend the evening and night at her best friend's home. The next day, her father was dead, shot point-blank in the head by his own hand. The date was December 6.

It was an unbearable shock for an eleven-year-old girl and her seven-year-old brother, despite all the years of abusive behavior that came out of endless bottles of alcohol. The horror of it didn't sink in until Kelly stole a peek through the window of the room where her father had met his violent end, and she recoiled at the sight of the blood-soaked walls and ceiling.

The guilt was even more unbearable. If she hadn't been so selfish, she would have seen her father at least one more time. Maybe if they'd gone to dinner, she and her brother, their father wouldn't have killed himself.

And then the shame set in. She was worthless. Not important enough for her father to stick around for. Not worth anything at all.

It didn't matter that her father's troubles were much bigger than she could comprehend; that he had been addicted to alcohol; or that his addiction had created a family life of misery.

Sometimes he was gone for days without explanation, and her mother would sit by cold dinners and weep without end. There would be screaming and fighting and assaults with pots and pans. The drinking drove Kelly's mother to desperation. Once, when Kelly was eight years old, she watched her mother slit her wrists. They were superficial cuts, a cry for attention, and Kelly's father rushed his wife to the hospital. When that attempt failed to change his ways, she tried again, by overdosing on pills. There was another rush to the hospital and her stomach was pumped. The children cowered at home alone all night.

When he took his life, a divorce was finally in progress. Even though he had found solace in another relationship, there was no peace for his soul in living, and so he tried to find it in death.

On January 17, just a little over a month after her father's suicide, the father of her best friend called her aside and asked, "How are you feeling about it now?" Little Kelly tried to be brave, and used the words she'd heard her mother say: "Oh, it's much better now, he's in peace, he doesn't have to drive us crazy." It wasn't how she felt at all.

The next day, the news came that her friend's dad had killed himself in the very same way— a shot to the head.

Wham wham. Two blows that shattered Kelly's very foundation.

Thus began the spiral downward, what Kelly later called "swirling the drain." The emptiness and the worthlessness grew bigger and bigger. The only thing that seemed to fill the space and keep the darkness away was numbness, and she found it in the wild life.

By the time she was in high school, Kelly was keeping company with a fast crowd. She started with alcohol and marijuana. It was the sophisticated thing to do in her small town—everyone who was cool did booze and drugs. At seventeen, she tried cocaine, and was a regular user at age nineteen. Life was getting high.

Kelly became involved with a man who shared her taste for drinking. They moved into a house together. They used drugs sparingly, and even gave them up for two years, but continued drinking. The relationship fell apart when her partner cheated on her. It was another blow to her already low self-esteem.

Kelly fled to her old friends and haunts. The friends had graduated to heavier drug usage, and she fell right into step with them.

By the time Kelly was twenty-three, she was thoroughly miserable, but had neither the motivation nor the strength to change her situation. She swirled the drain, going down deeper and deeper into a bottomless pit of unhappiness. The next drink, the next line of cocaine would hold the misery at bay for a while. She was able to keep a job, but night after night, she went out drinking and then dragged herself to work hungover. She called in sick often.

The year that she turned twenty-three, on the night before Christmas Eve, Kelly was partying as usual. At about 10 or 11 P.M., she and four friends set out to drink at a neighborhood bar in Milwaukee that Kelly had never been to before. They arrived at a nearly empty establishment. There were three people seated in a far corner. Kelly and her friends took a table near the bar and got themselves drinks. Hers was a screwdriver.

Finishing her drink, she went to the ladies' room and snorted a small amount of coke. She returned to her table and resumed chatting with her friends. The bar was still nearly empty. One of the friends handed her some money and said, "Here, get us some more drinks." She took everybody's order and turned to go to the bartender, who was working behind the bar.

Suddenly she noticed that a large black man with a balding head was seated at the bar. *Where did he come from?* Kelly thought, wondering how she had missed his entrance. Plus, it was unusual to see people of color in this particular part of town.

The man looked straight at her with the most compelling, magnetizing eyes she had ever seen. A mug of beer, full right to the brim and frothy as though freshly poured, sat in front of him.

She had the impression that he was kind. The thought made her feel odd. How could she possibly know that? He was a total stranger.

The man started talking to her in a low voice that was hard to hear.

"What?" she said.

He waved her over to him. When she was closer, he said quietly, "You don't need to do that." He pointed to the bottles of liquor behind the bar.

Kelly looked at him, puzzled.

"You know what you need to do," the man said firmly. "You're hurting yourself, and that isn't what God wants you to do. There is a reason you are here and there are things that you need to do."

How does he know anything about me? Kelly thought. She wasn't alarmed, however. The man had a comforting presence, and it seemed like the most natural thing to stand there and talk to him. "What do you mean?" she asked. "What things?"

"You'll see," he answered vaguely. "But you can't continue on the path you are going. It's not where you are meant to be."

Kelly continued talking to the man. The surroundings of the bar faded away. Time seemed to stand still. He seemed to know so much about her. Talking to him was like talking to a father, the kind she never had, one who made her feel enveloped in unconditional love.

Everything he said hit the target about how Kelly was wasting her life. About her feelings of worthlessness. About her guilt over her father's suicide. The man wasn't at all judgmental. Rather, he offered words of wisdom, hope, and encouragement that resonated deeply within her soul, touching a truth.

After what seemed like a long time—but turned out to be only a few minutes—Kelly walked back to her table of friends. "Hey, where's our drinks?" one of them wanted to know.

She started to tell them about the strange man at the bar. She turned to point—but no one was there. The man had mysteriously vanished. A full mug of beer, untouched, sat alone on the bar countertop.

Kelly's friends hooted with laughter.

"But there's his beer!" she protested.

More gales of laughter. There had been no big, bald black man sitting at the bar, they insisted. They would have seen him. "You're crazy!" they told her.

A queer feeling passed through Kelly. The thought crossed her mind that perhaps this was no ordinary man. Maybe he was an agent of God. Was he an angel? Had God reached out to her and spoken to her?

Kelly let the matter drop and tried to resume the holiday merrymaking with her friends. She ordered more drinks. As she drank into the night, the image of the strange man refused to go away. She wanted to remember every word he had spoken, but most vanished like wisps of dreams.

But the essence of what he said stayed with her, and affected her deeply. Kelly knew he was right. She had to take responsibility for herself, take action to change her life. She couldn't change the past. She couldn't change other people. She could only change herself.

Kelly thought about angels. She believed in angels, though she had never expected to encounter one. Especially in a bar. Weren't angels supposed to have wings and be obvious? But if angels were real and God did use them to talk to people, wouldn't they go to a place where they were likely to find you? Wouldn't they seem like a friendly person? Kelly had to admit that the place she most likely could be found would be at a bar or a party.

The man most definitely had to have been an angel. His eyes were so unusual, so compelling. Kelly had never seen eyes like that in a person. He knew too much about her. He said just the right things—a spiritual message that went straight to the core of her being.

Within days Kelly called an addictions treatment center and was put on a waiting list. She was admitted about a month later. Initially it was hard for her to stay in the program. She looked at others there, and thought them worse off and more desperate. *They* were the ones who needed treatment, not she. But soon she saw the desperation and need in herself, and stayed.

With the help of that program and Alcoholics Anonymous, Kelly got herself clean, straight, and sober. She was able to reclaim her self-worth and self-esteem, and see herself as a good person who deserved to be loved, and who had a lot of love to give and many accomplishments to achieve in the world. Three years later, she met a wonderful man through AA. They fell in love, got married, and became the happy parents of two children.

A decade has passed since that fateful Christmas, and Kelly still thinks about the mysterious black man. She knows without a doubt he was her personal angel, come to make her look into a mirror of truth. He saved her life.

She has often wished that she could find him and thank him, but—in the fashion of angels and the mysterious workings of divine intervention—he has never been seen since. Instead, his work carries on through Kelly, who has become an angel to others. She shares her story of adversity and triumph, planting the seeds of hope and encouragement that enable others to break free of their prisons of addiction and find the happiness that is rightfully theirs.

I Will Be
Your Rock

From the day Adison was born, it was apparent that a very special bond existed between her and her proud grandfather, Ken, whom Adison called Poppy. With her long strawberry blond hair, sparkling blue eyes, and dimpled chin, she was the portrait of a little angel. She had big, chubby cheeks just like Poppy. He'd laugh and squeeze her cheeks, and she would laugh and reach up and squeeze his. The family joked that she was the only one who was allowed to squeeze Poppy's cheeks.

At her birth, he gave Adi a little toy horse that ran in circles. As she got older, it was far and away her favorite toy. Whenever Adison's parents, Dawn and Brian, took her to visit her grandparents, Adi always looked for Poppy first. If he wasn't immediately in sight as soon as she came in the door, she would call, "Where's Poppy? Where's Poppy?"

All Poppy had to do was give a special look and Adi would laugh and giggle. If Adi was crying or upset, Ken would lay her on his chest, and she would immediately calm down.

One December 12, Dawn made plans to meet her parents for lunch at a shopping mall. It was a big event—Adi's first Santa visit and first Christmas.

Ken returned to work after lunch. At the office, he noticed blood in his urine, and called his doctor.

By December 17, he was in surgery to have a cancerous kidney removed.

The suddenness and magnitude of the situation was a staggering shock for the family. Ken was an athletic, energetic man in his early fifties, enjoying the prime of his life. Now he was lying on an operating table, faced with one of the rarest and deadliest of cancers, one that does not respond to conventional chemotherapy or radiation.

The initial outlook was optimistic, however, for the indications were that the cancer was still encapsulated in his kidney. An operation might be able to remove all of the cancer.

But the operation went on much longer than expected. A sinking feeling settled over the anxious family that perhaps doctors had found the cancer had spread.

Ken went home from the hospital on December 23, his prognosis still uncertain while further tests were done on lymph node biopsies. He insisted that he didn't want to change the traditional Christmas plans for a family gathering. A hospital bed was set up in the living room, and nearly two dozen family members—including Dawn's sister, Dana, and brother, Michael—gathered to give thanks for being together. A buffet potluck replaced Charlotte's sit-down dinner, freeing her from cooking.

As ever, Ken was especially delighted to see Adi. She had a gift for Poppy: a rock she had picked up from their driveway on the way into the house. She deposited it in his hands. Dawn looked at her puzzled father. "She insisted on picking up this rock for you," was all she could offer by way of explanation. He smiled and said, "Well, she's going to be my rock."

It was the last Christmas the family would spend together. A few days later, word came that the cancer had indeed spread to Ken's lymph nodes.

Dawn, an epidemiologist, was given time off from work to research treatment options. She discovered that most were experimental and some programs required qualification. Ken traveled around the country to leading hospitals and treatment centers, trying different therapies. By January, the cancer was in his lungs, disqualifying him from one particular trial therapy.

As the cancer progressed, Ken kept working at his job and strove to maintain as normal a life as possible. Whenever Dawn brought Adison for a visit, the little girl now insisted on carrying in a rock from the driveway as a gift. If Dawn said no, Adi threw a temper tantrum until her mother relented. Whenever she went on hikes with Dawn and Brian, she meticulously searched for rocks for Poppy. Adi gave Poppy so many rocks that Charlotte bought a special basket for all of them. Sometimes she gave him three or four rocks at a time.

With horrifying speed, the cancer raced through Ken's body. In June, it spread to his brain, and he suffered a stroke. Doctors said it was unlikely that he would recover or ever walk again, but Ken had more willpower than that: He was up and walking within seven days.

Soon, however, even Ken's tremendous will was no match for the cancer, which spread to his liver. In August, death was nearing. The family was together as much as possible, doing everything they could to make his transition peaceful and comfortable. Dawn, Dana, and Michael stayed overnight during the last weeks of Ken's life. Ken was concerned about how the family would fare after he was gone, especially with things that needed to be done to the house. Specifically, the roof needed fixing, and he hadn't been able to get it done. Two days before Ken died, Brian and Michael eased his worries by fixing the roof.

Right to the end, Ken defied his disease. The family was told to expect him to lose his ability to communicate and to lapse into a coma. But on his last day, August 20, he was awake and aware, listening to audiotapes of the children when they were young.

In the evening, his breathing became labored, and then increasingly so. The family gathered around Ken, and with their mother, they prayed the rosary, held his hand, and told him how much they loved him. They gave him permission to go, assuring him that though there would be many tears, they would continue to live by the example he set. At last he took one great breath, and was gone.

At that very instant, a loud thump sounded on the roof. "He's checking your work," Dawn said to Brian and Michael, and everyone laughed. It broke the unbearable sadness. Earlier, Dana had told her dad that one of his greatest gifts was his ability to make others laugh, no matter how much pain they were in. Once again, he had succeeded.

The next day when Brian arrived at Ken and Charlotte's home with Adison, she did not automatically pick up a rock. Adi had never been told that Poppy was going to die, and she hadn't yet been told that he was gone.

"Where's Poppy?" she asked, not spying him immediately.

"He's gone," said Dawn, preparing to tell Adi the news.

"Gone to heaven?" asked Adi without a prompt.

"Why, yes," answered Dawn, astonished that she would know.

The funeral was three days later. When Dawn, Brian, and Adi returned to their own home, Dawn found a large rock sitting right in the middle of their bed. It was about four inches long by three inches wide, not the sort of little stone that gets caught in a shoe and finds its way indoors. Right away Dawn knew that it was a sign from her father.

Rocks began turning up in strange places: in the living room, the bathroom, on Adi's car seat. Once Dawn got out the vacuum cleaner, turned it on, and heard a rattling inside. It was a rock. So many rocks turned up that she had to get a special basket for them. The basket joined Poppy's basket of rocks. Other rocks were found beside their beds. Where the rocks came from remained a mystery, as the driveway and road in front of the house were asphalt. The rocks appeared especially when Dawn was feeling sad and missing her father, or when she was having a bad day. The message that always came to Dawn when she found a rock was that her father was going to be their rock now, like a guardian angel.

One of the most dramatic episodes occurred after Dawn had a special ring made for herself—and to eventually pass on to Adison—with a large citrine gem set in it. Citrine was Ken's birthstone. One evening, Dawn went to a concert in downtown Baltimore with her mother and sister. After returning home, she realized that the citrine was missing. Heartbroken, she assumed it had been lost downtown. She and Brian searched through the house just in case it had fallen out there. Brian also thoroughly searched the car that evening. He searched it again in the morning. The stone was gone.

The next day, Dawn was in the yard gardening when an inner voice prompted her, "Go look in the car." She opened her car door, and there in the center of the driver's seat rested the citrine. Dawn looked up and said, "Thanks, Dad!"

For Adison, Poppy remained as present and as accessible as he was in life. She often said she could see him, and that he came to her at night and gave her hugs and kisses. They played together, and once, Adi said with great gravity, she read him a book. On some mornings after she awakened, she would relay little bits of their conversations from the night before. She would blurt out, "Hi, Poppy!" and point to where she could see him: sometimes in the room and sometimes out the window in the yard. She wanted her favorite toy, the little horse, with her most of the time, and even took it to bed.

The most profound evidence of Adi's continued contact with her Poppy occurred one night during the Christmas season the following year. Adi was now nearly two years old. Fifteen minutes after putting her to bed, Dawn heard Adison cheering. She crept up to her door and listened. Adi was shouting, "Yeah! Poppy's here! Yeah, Poppy!" Dawn desperately wanted to open the door—perhaps she could behold what Adi saw—but she kept her hand from turning the knob. She let Adi and Poppy play. Adi sang some songs, including the "I Love You" song popularized by Barney the purple dinosaur. Then the room grew quiet and it was evident that Adi had gone to sleep.

When Brian came home, he took one look at the wide-eyed expression of wonder on Dawn's face and asked with alarm, "What happened?"

"It's amazing," Dawn proclaimed, and proceeded to explain what she'd heard.

The next morning, Dawn asked Adi, "What happened in your room last night?"

"Poppy was here," Adi said. "He gave me hugs and kisses."

Adison's experiences with Poppy and her comments comforted the family. Once when Charlotte was sad, Adi asked her grandmother, "What's the matter, Gee?"

"I miss Poppy," Charlotte said.

"Poppy's here, Gee Gee," exclaimed Adison.

"Where?" questioned Charlotte.

"Right in this room. Everywhere!"

Indeed, Poppy was everywhere. Life in the body ends, but love never ends. There are no boundaries between hearts.

EveRlasting

LOve

Comfort

Ken

Lost
and Found

$\mathcal{J}$ason* was home for the Christmas holiday. Home was the inner city in Newark, New Jersey, where rows of deteriorated tenements made powerful statements of poverty, despair, and broken dreams. Jason had spent his childhood growing up here, clinging to one solemn vow: that he would escape the inner city, be a self-made man of success, and come back to help his family and others. He was closer to realizing that dream now, for a church scholarship program had enabled him to start college. It was his freshman year.

The neighborhood kids were excited to see Jason. Most looked up to him. If he could go to college, so could they.

Jason was inspired to organize something fun for the children as a small Christmas gift. They seldom got out of their neighborhood. He asked

* All names have been changed.

them what they'd like to do most, and they answered, "Go to the zoo!" The Bronx Zoo was not far away. It seemed an odd excursion for December, but the weather was mild. Okay, Jason decided. They would go to the zoo. It would be a great outing. They could travel by subway and bus, leave on a Saturday morning, and be home by late afternoon.

Before he knew it, Jason had ten children ranging in age from nine to thirteen to join him on his "Christmas Zoo Expedition."

To help him keep track of ten excited and restless children, Jason drafted his younger brother, Craig, to come along. Together they set out with the children, herding them along the streets, onto the right bus, and down into the subway to the right train. At the zoo, it was a challenge to monitor all the kids, who darted off in various directions every time something captured their attention.

Nonetheless, everyone had a splendid time. The children moaned and protested when Jason told them it was time to start home.

But as they headed toward the subway, Jason found himself disoriented. They boarded a train and got off at a stop that Jason thought was the correct one, and walked up to the street level. To his surprise and chagrin, he discovered that Craig was no longer with them. Somehow his brother had gotten separated from the group.

The street surroundings looked unfamiliar, and rather unfriendly as well. There are portions of the Bronx in which it is not wise to linger. Suddenly, Jason wasn't sure where they were. He asked several passersby for directions; they all gave conflicting answers. *This is no help at all,* he thought. He didn't want to alarm the children, so he said, "Let's keep walking for a while," in as calm a voice as he could manage.

Jason continued to stop people and ask them for directions. Sometimes he got nothing more than shrugs and blank looks.

Just as he was beginning to feel desperate, Jason spied a young man coming toward them on the sidewalk. He had bright red, curly hair and shining blue eyes, and walked with a light and jaunty step.

"Sir, can you—" Jason began.

The red-haired young man cut him off. "Follow me," he said gruffly.

"But wait, I need directions—"

"I know," said Curly Top.

Jason was mystified. How could this stranger know what he needed— where he needed to go? He kept trying to explain, but every time he began a sentence, Curly Top cut him off with "I know where you're going."

Jason shook his head. He wasn't going to argue—he had ten kids to get home safely, and he was in uncertain territory. He motioned to the children, and they all followed Curly Top down the street as though he were the Pied Piper of the Bronx.

After several blocks, Curly Top darted down a subway staircase. He stopped on the platform and pointed to a track, indicating that it was one that would get everyone home.

Jason turned around for a brief moment to tell the children. Then he turned around to thank his mysterious helper.

But the man was gone. Simply vanished as though into thin air. "Where did he go?" asked Jason. But none of the children could tell him. Nobody knew.

Jason and the children arrived back home safely. So did Craig. When Craig asked Jason what had happened, he said, "I'm not sure, but I think we were rescued by an angel!"

It was a flip remark, and they laughed. But the words stuck in Jason's mind. Maybe "angel" wasn't a joke. He'd learned about angels in church, of course. Those angels seemed very remote to him. He'd seen a few television programs about angels intervening in the lives of people to help them sort out their problems. Those were nice stories, but did such things really happen in life?

As if in answer to his musings, Jason keep coming across angels: books about angels, shows about angels. People made remarks about angels. It was as though the universe were trying to send him a message. Angels seemed to be everywhere.

One night Jason was sitting in front of the television surfing the channels with the remote control. He stopped when he heard the word *angels*. A woman was talking. The tag line identified her as an author of a book about angels.

"We think angels have to be big beings of light, but actually they are more likely to appear to us as regular human beings," the woman was saying. "If you were in a jam and some enormous winged thing came swooping down out of the sky, you'd be terrified. But if you're approached by what appears to be a friendly person, you're going to listen. You're going to be grateful for the help."

Her next words struck Jason like lightning:

"Angels give us directions for all things in life," she said. "They always know what you need and where you need to go."

Keep Your Intention on God

$\mathcal{A}$ nasty ice storm was brewing as Reverend Toni G. Boehm finished teaching her prayer class and prepared to leave work for the day. She looked out into the darkening sky at the rain mixed with sleet and freezing rain. Just a short while before, it had only been raining. Now the roads would be slick and difficult to drive on.

To make matters worse, Toni couldn't drive straight home. Tonight her sister, Sonny, was flying in to visit for the holidays, and Toni had promised to pick her up. What a dreadful night to drive the forty miles out to the Kansas City airport!

Despite the storm, Toni wasn't too worried about the trip. Though her Lincoln Town Car didn't have front-wheel drive, it was a big, heavy car. And, the prayer class had left her in a clear and calm state of mind. She was looking forward to seeing Sonny.

As Toni collected her belongings, she became aware of an inner voice that said, *Keep your intention on God.* She was accustomed to receiving such inner guidance—the voice of the angels speaking to her. As founder of the Awakening Hearts Ministry and an accomplished spiritual teacher, Toni had devoted much of her life to the soul's path to Oneness. She prayed and meditated daily, and strove to hear and follow the divine guidance.

Toni knew immediately that the message pertained to driving. She answered silently, *What do you want me to do?*

The inner voice said, *Keep your mind focused on God by using these words: "Kadoish kadoish kadoish, Adonai 'Tsebayoth."*

Toni recognized the Hebrew words as from the book of Revelation: "Holy holy holy is the Lord God of Hosts." Oddly, she couldn't recall ever hearing the words spoken, yet they rang clearly in her mind. They sounded like an ancient mantra of power and protection. She said to herself, *All right, I will do that.*

Toni silently repeated the words over and over as she started up her car and eased out onto the highway. She kept repeating them as she felt tension tighten within her. The road conditions were far worse than she'd imagined, and were deteriorating with every passing minute. Long stretches of road were as slick as an ice rink. Travel was slow and painstaking.

Toni crept along the freeway in the right lane, her hands clenched around the steering wheel. The speedometer hovered at 15 to 20 miles an hour. Even that seemed too fast for the treacherous conditions. The headlights barely penetrated the wind-whipped sleet and freezing rain. The windshield wipers worked furiously. The defroster hummed on high. It seemed that at any moment, the storm would gain the advantage and the car would be engulfed. There were no other vehicles on the road. Toni was alone on what seemed the highway to hell.

At last she saw that she had about ten more miles to go. It was the home stretch. She couldn't let down her guard, however. The last few miles to the airport were in an isolated area, and if a mishap happened here, it might be a long time before anyone would come along.

Toni looked into the rearview mirror and saw two dim yellow lights in the distance behind her. So someone else was unlucky enough to be driving on a night like this!

The lights grew closer, and Toni could make out the shape of a large tractor-trailer truck. The lights swung to the left and the truck pulled ahead. Then she saw that there was a second tractor-trailer behind the first. It too pulled to the left to pass her.

Both trucks then pulled back into the slow lane one ahead of the other, both directly in front of Toni. To her annoyance, slush from the back wheels of the truck spewed out in front of her. "Of all the nerve! What if they throw up rocks that hit the car and damage it?" she fumed aloud. How very inconsiderate! Why couldn't they have passed on and kept going in the left lane?

Preoccupied with the trucks, Toni stopped repeating her affirmation. She made the decision to speed up and go around them. She pulled over into the left lane and stepped on the gas.

As she passed the truck directly in front of her, her accelerating car hit a patch of ice. Suddenly she was spinning crazily out of control. She flew past the truck toward the lead truck. In a split second, Toni saw that she was heading for a crash with the back end of the lead truck. The realization that she would surely be smashed between the trucks and killed flashed through her mind. Her thoughts screamed: *There's no way I'm going to get out of this!*

In the same instant, a radiant light filled the entire car. Toni felt something in the midst of the light—a presence—literally take hold of the steering wheel. What happened next seemed to pass in agonizing slow motion.

Toni's car slid past the end of the truck, so close that it seemed a hair couldn't squeeze between the two vehicles. Her car spun around again and dropped into a gully at the edge of the freeway. She was facing in the opposite direction.

The trucks continued on, their drivers oblivious, their red taillights dwindling in size as they vanished into the stormy night.

Toni rested against the steering wheel, heart pounding. One moment she had been certain she was about to die, and the next moment she was safe in a gully. The entire episode had all happened in the blink of an eye.

And what was that presence? An angel? The radiance was gone, but a faint electrical quality hung in the air.

She would think about it later. Right now, she had to get out of this gully. She had to make it safely to the airport. Steadying herself, Toni turned the ignition. *Sonny... I've got to get Sonny.*

But when she stepped on the accelerator, the car lurched a bit and then stalled. She tried it again and got the same results. There was too much ice and slush for the car to clear the sharp incline out of the gully.

Toni fought back the panic that threatened to seize her as her darkest fear materialized. "What am I going to do?" she said, peering out her frosted windows into the darkness. She had no cellular phone, and was miles from a service area. She thought about her husband, Jay, who was back at home, unaware of her plight. It would be some time before her undue absence would be a cause for alarm. "There's nobody on the road—who's going to find me?"

The affirmation surfaced again, shouldering away the fear: *Keep your intention on God.* The words rang in her mind. Again she heard the inner voice: *Those trucks were your gift. They were warming the road for you.* Toni swallowed hard as the truth burst upon her. The trucks that had irritated her had instead been clearing a path for her. If she had stayed behind them, she would have been fine. They had been sent as a gift from God—a gift she had failed to recognize.

Humbled, Toni acknowledged the gift. She then prayed for the ability to get to the airport. She turned the key on the ignition again, and put the car in gear. Gently she pressed the accelerator, then more firmly. The car lifted up and over the incline. She was out of the gully and back on the shoulder of the road.

For the remaining ten miles of the journey, Toni kept her eyes on the road and her intention on God. She repeated her mantra prayer, "Kadoish

kadoish kadoish, Adonai 'Tsebayoth." Holy holy holy is the Lord God of Hosts.

When she reached the airport, relief surged through her. She parked the car and dashed through the driving sleet and freezing rain into the terminal. She ran straight for a telephone and called the Silent Unity prayer line. She sobbed out her brush with death and was comforted and steadied by the prayers offered in response.

Sonny's plane landed safely. The journey back to Toni's home was slow but without incident. Never had the Christmas lights winking from the house looked so welcoming. Never was she so glad to see Jay open the door. But for an angel's hand, she might never have looked into his eyes or felt his loving embrace again.

It was not until after the holiday activities had passed that the full measure of Toni's experience settled upon her. She thought about death looming before her in a split second, and the miraculous angelic presence that had steered her car to safety.

She also felt permanently changed in a deep and profound way. Not just because she had come so close to death, but also because she had missed the gift of God. Rather than allow her journey to unfold as guided by a divine hand, she had taken charge herself with the trucks. She had assumed that she knew the best course of action—but succeeded only in jeopardizing herself and others.

Toni wondered, *How much more in life am I missing because I put myself in charge instead of God?* How many other times had God opened the way for her, laid a gift at her door that she left unrecognized? How many opportunities had been passed, solutions to problems ignored?

It would never be that way again. Toni resolved to pay greater heed to her guidance. To live more fully in the moment, appreciating the glory that is life. And to have faith in the fact that the eyes of God see the greater plan, while the eyes of humankind see a more limited horizon. God prepares the way for all living things. No storm need defeat us if we but keep our intention focused upon God.

A Heavenly
Doctor Makes
a House Call

The day after Christmas, a blizzard hit Detroit. Everyone stayed indoors; nothing moved on the streets. The blizzard raged on into the night.

Around 10 P.M., Vondalyn descended the basement steps to her bedroom in the house. She didn't see a bottle that had been left on the steps. Her foot landed on it, twisted, and she spun off balance, falling and landing her entire weight—some 280 pounds—on her right ankle. The pain was excruciating.

Her family rushed to her assistance and tried to help her to her bed. But it hurt too much to move, and Vondalyn told them to leave her on the steps and call for emergency services. She wondered how anyone could reach her in the midst of the blizzard. She might be stuck on these steps, in severe pain, all night.

Vondalyn began to pray. She prayed to all of her ancestors who had even the smallest connection to medicine and healing. She kept up constant prayer. Then she prayed to St. Luke, the patron saint of physicians. The prayer made both the pain and the waiting bearable.

After some time had passed—Vondalyn was not sure how much—she felt invisible hands examine her from head to toe. A male voice distinctly told her, "Hold your right ankle very still. Do not let it dangle." The voice was soothing. It told her over and over, "Relax. You will be fine."

But Vondalyn began to slip into shock. The voice remained calm, and told her to instruct someone to wrap her in a blanket.

She looked over at one of the basement walls. Standing there was what appeared to be a person—with wings. She could not see it clearly. It was in shadow, except there was nothing in the room to cast shadows there.

The emergency crew eventually arrived at the house. When they checked Vondalyn, they found that all of her vital signs were normal. "You did everything right," they told her.

Vondalyn's ankle was broken in two places and was dislocated. Surgery was required, followed by an order for plenty of bedrest. Doctors told her that it would take about four months for her ankle to mend properly.

Vondalyn was discharged from physical therapy after only six visits, and she was back at work in two months. She never even required pain medication.

Vondalyn knew why she healed so quickly. Someone was with her that night, someone angelic.

Perhaps it was Raphael himself, the archangel of healing.

The
Christmas
Wish

The most important thing in Bea Sheftel's world was family. Sharing, caring, and loving, helping each other out in the bad times, celebrating with each other in the good times. Family had always come first for Bea.

Christmas was always a special time, the happiest day of the year. Bea loved the holiday season, its lights, decorations, music, and joy. She especially loved sharing all that with her family. Bea hailed from a close-knit Italian clan, and it just wasn't Christmas without everyone together. But this year, Christmas loomed as a time of emptiness and loneliness for Bea and her husband of thirty-five years, Bruce.

The week before Christmas, they were saddened by the unexpected death of Bruce's aunt Geri. Dr. Geraldine Lynne was a good friend who had been like a member of the family for more than fifty years, and had acquired the honorary title of "Aunt" Geri. Everyone was so proud of her because she was the first woman doctor to head a hospital. In her early career, she delivered most of the babies in the family. Her passing left a hole for the holiday that would not be filled. Added to that was the absence of Bea's aunt Kathryn, who had moved to Arizona.

Then Bea's only son, Rob, broke the news that he had other plans for Christmas. Bea's brother announced he was going away for the holidays. And her sister was uncertain about making the drive to Connecticut to join them.

It broke Bea's heart. Her parents were both gone, having died years before. Her mother's dying wish had been for her family not to drift apart, and Bea had always looked upon herself as the one who kept everyone together. This would mark the first Christmas in which the entire family went separate ways.

As December 25 approached, Bea tried to find the happiness in the season, anyway. She and Bruce attended a wonderful Christmas concert, presented by a choir whose members came from different churches. Their singing was delightful and inspiring, and Bea, Bruce, and the rest of the audience joined in singing favorite Christmas carols. It reminded Bea of happy family Christmases past. They left in good spirits.

The next day, Bea and Bruce had breakfast with their friends Steve and Lucy, and did some Christmas shopping at the mall. Steve said he planned to spend Christmas Day with his sister. Lucy planned to stay home alone. She had lost her husband some years before, and it was still difficult to be with other families on Christmas Day.

Bea's Christmas shopping always included gifts for charity and others in need, and this year was no exception. If someone were to ask Bea what she wanted to be other than a writer, she'd say, "I wish I were a philanthropist!" She wasn't rich, but she always gave what she could, knowing that even small gifts make a big difference.

At the mall, she and Bruce picked a name from the Giving Tree. The request was for a sweatshirt for someone at the Salvation Army homeless shelter. Bea bought the size specified and left it at the tree.

They bought gifts for the four young children of a dear friend, Jim, who had died the previous year. They dropped off donations of craft supplies from Bea's craft shop for a hospital Christmas gift sale. They also bought new toys to donate to a television station's Toys for Tots drive.

But even the joy of helping others still did not fill the emptiness that lay ahead for Christmas Day itself. The one gift that Bea wanted—simply to be gathered together with her family and dearest friends—was not to be had. She and Bruce would be alone, and suddenly it seemed that this was the beginning of many lonely holidays ahead.

For solace, Bea turned to prayer. She knew the power of prayer, especially since the time of her father's first heart attack. She also knew the power and presence of angels, and often felt her own guardian angel around her. She asked her angel now for guidance, not sure how to pray about the coming Christmas. She remembered how it had been with her father, Salvatore, during his last days.

· · ·

Sal lived his entire life in his native Brooklyn, New York. After his wife, Frances, died, he lived alone, visited and aided by his family and friends. He was a solid man, warmhearted, and a soft touch. For twenty-five years, he worked in the adoption courts and loved children. In turn, children loved him, and called him "Papa Sal." Bea adored him.

One day he had a heart attack. At the time, the family was scattered. Bea and her sister, Ginny, were in Arizona visiting relatives. Her husband,

Bruce, was in Virginia visiting his brother and sister-in-law. Her son, Rob, was in Connecticut. Her brother, Richard, was the only one in New York, out on Long Island. He was the one who took Sal to the hospital.

They all went immediately to Sal's side. They were advised that he would not survive.

Deeply shaken, Bea went to Mass and offered it for her father. She didn't know how she should pray. Should she ask for her father to live? She desperately wanted him to live, but didn't know what was best for him. She decided to ask for God's grace and blessings upon his life, and for God's will. The prayer filled her with a certainty that Sal would recover. She told her brother and sister, "Don't believe Dad is going to die."

"Prepare yourself," they answered.

"No, Dad will live." Bea felt the assurance in her heart.

One day Bea visited Sal and found him moved out of critical care into a private room. Her cousin, Father Francis, a priest, and the hospital chaplain were administering the Catholic sacrament of laying on of hands. "This is the answer to my prayers!" Bea exclaimed. From that day on, Sal healed quickly.

After Sal improved enough to leave the hospital, the children had to find a nursing home for him since he was still weak and needed more care than they could give him in any of their homes. Bea searched for one in Connecticut, though her siblings told her that Sal would never want to leave his beloved Brooklyn.

Bea prayed to Padre Pio, *Please bring Dad to me so that I can look after him.*

Bea found a nursing home a few minutes from her house in Connecticut. She visited him every day and helped him regain some of the physical and mental abilities he had lost. At first he didn't remember who was who among the grandchildren. So, Bea made up photo albums and went over the pictures with him day after day until he knew for sure which grandchildren belonged to which of his children. With a wheelchair, Bruce and Bea took him out at night to eat, to go to the mall, and to their home. Sal especially loved going to the mall to watch the children. They also went to country fairs, craft shows, musical programs, and plays. Bea's brother and sister took turns traveling from New York to visit Sal, too.

Bea worked with her dad during physical therapy. He graduated from the wheelchair to a walker. The walker was hard for him. When Bea pleaded with the therapy staff for a cane, they told her they'd done their best, and she should be happy with the progress he had made. Bea prayed, "God, I'd love for Dad to be able to walk with a quad cane."

Out of the blue, Aunt Kit sent Bea a quad cane she'd bought at a tag sale. The nursing home wouldn't help Sal learn how to use it, so Bea worked with him. Soon he did very well and then went to a plain cane, and finally to no cane at all. A year had passed since his heart attack. More than anything, pure love from his family had healed Sal.

Bea shopped for an independent retirement apartment for her father, and moved him out of the nursing home. She and Bruce visited him every weekend, and Bea visited during the week, when her friend Steve would drive her. Sal especially enjoyed these visits, because he and Steve could have lively talks about politics. Bea took him to all his medical appointments, and saw him through two cataract operations.

At Christmastime, Sal told Bea, "This is your place. Decorate it any way you want." She went wild, creating a holiday wonderland. She decorated the tree with handmade ornaments, many created by Bea and others acquired from craft shows. There was a Nativity scene, and a display of stuffed animals. Sal's favorites were a red bear from Bea, which said "I love you" when squeezed, and a moose that bellowed, "Ho ho ho, Merry Christmas" when squeezed. Every available space, including the windowsills, was covered with decorations and lights. Sal loved the decorations so much he insisted that they stay up until the end of January.

Sal made many friends in the retirement community, and was happy. Every time Bea visited him, she'd find him sitting in his wing chair. He'd point to his cheek and say, "Where's my kiss?" Bea would give him a big kiss. They would visit, maybe take a walk to the lake outside the building, or take a ride. The times they shared were some of the best and closest times Bea had had with her dad since she was a little girl.

But the sweetness did not last forever, nor could it. At age eighty-six, Sal had a second heart attack and was taken to the hospital. Doctors said an operation might save his life. But the gentle old man developed pneumonia. He was being kept alive solely by machines.

Bea was praying for her father when she felt the presence of her angel and heard in her heart the angel's words: *You must help your father ease from this life to the next.*

Bea's answer was silent, spoken from the heart as she sobbed. *I can't do that. Please, I can't do that. I don't want my father to die. I'll take care of him,* she pleaded.

The angel said, *You won't be alone. This is to be your last gift to your father. You must pray with him because he cannot speak. You are to help him go over to the other side and release him.*

Bea knew that because he and she were so close, he would not want to leave if she did not want him to leave. She knew that it was at last his time to go, and her prayers would not save him.

She got her Bible and read from Psalms. She prayed with her father as she had never prayed before. She talked about his mother and how she was waiting for him on the other side, and how she missed him. She talked about her mother, Frances, and the others who had gone on, and how they were all waiting for him. She let her father go. It was the hardest thing Bea had ever done in her life.

Bea called a priest for last rites. As the ritual was performed, she felt such an elation, a freeing of the spirit that made her rejoice. She turned to the priest and asked, "Did you feel that?" He only looked at her quizzically.

Her sister and her family, her brother and his wife, Rob, Bruce, and Bea were together in Sal's room the night he died. They tenderly said their good-byes. As the life-support system was unhooked, they kissed him one last time. Bea thought her heart would burst. But she had done as her angel had asked her.

That first Christmas without him, Bea pasted her house with his pictures so she could feel him close by. He was with her.

In fact, Bea often felt the presences of Sal and Frances in addition to her guardian angel. They were like guardian angels to her. She would pray to her guardian angel, *Please tell my parents I love them.*

·   ·   ·

Now, thinking of her lonely Christmas, Bea didn't pray to God to change Rob's mind about spending the day away—she knew that wouldn't be right. Perhaps she was being selfish by wanting others to be with her on Christmas Day. Bea asked God to forgive her for being selfish, and prayed to her guardian angel to help her not be selfish. She reminded her angel how she had taken care of her father and how she had loved him, and that all she wanted was her family. Was that wrong?

Sometimes Bea could feel her angel laughing, and then she knew the problem she was bringing to the angel's attention was solved and she need not worry. Even though she was sad about Christmas, she had the feeling now of her angel smiling with the reassurance that everything would be okay. She took it to mean that she should enjoy the day with her husband. Perhaps they would go out to eat, she thought. Cooking a meal would only remind her of who was absent from the house.

Christmas morning dawned. Bea awakened with the feeling that Sal and Frances were in the room, as real as if they were in the flesh. She knew that they'd heard her prayer in her heart. They hovered above her as she lay in bed. "We have a gift for you," they told her. "We're giving you your Christmas wish. Merry Christmas!" Bea felt her sadness instantly vanish and her heart lift with love.

Soon Rob came over and said his plans had changed—he would spend the day with them. Bea was beside herself with joy. Then Steve called and said his sister had decided to go to a friend's home. Bea told him, "Get on over here." Steve joined the little party.

Bea cooked up a big meal. It was just like old times. They opened gifts. They watched the traditional Christmas shows on TV. They played games. Bea and Rob played with Rob's new hockey game and video games while Bruce and Steve talked. Throughout the day, Bea's smile was brighter than the lights on the Christmas tree. But the gift of family didn't end with that marvelous Christmas day.

Bea's sister came the day after Christmas. And her nephew Bill came up from New York to spend New Year's weekend in the area. Bill announced that he and his fiancée, Dyana, were going to buy a house in Connecticut, near both his mother in New York and Bea—"so we can be together as a family!" That was the icing on the cake for Bea. She jumped up and down with happiness at the news. Bill laughed.

What had threatened to be a sad Christmas turned out to be the best, thanks to a prayer, an angel, and the loving angels of a mother and father. The family was together, and Bea felt very blessed.

Peace,
Be Still

One day shortly before Christmas, Juliet found a lump in her left breast. The diagnosis was cancer, and an immediate operation was necessary.

The doctor said she had two options. One was a total mastectomy. The second was a partial mastectomy, followed by radiation and chemotherapy. Juliet was eighty-one years of age, and was not heartened by the prospect of near-toxic drugs and radiation. The side effects were debilitating, and she juggled a full schedule for her various charitable activities.

"Go home and think about it," urged the doctor. "But let me know tomorrow."

She looked at him and said, "There are only three people who really care whether I have a mastectomy."

The doctor looked startled. Three people?

Juliet went on to explain that the three were her pussycats, who loved to curl up at her bosom to sleep at night.

Juliet decided to have a total mastectomy. It was scheduled immediately. When she entered the hospital, a friend gave her a little brass-colored metal angel to hang over her bed as a good luck and comfort charm. The haloed angel was blowing a trumpet, like a miniature Gabriel heralding news. Juliet fell in love with it, and when the time came for her to leave the hospital, she took it home to hang over her own bed.

Juliet had not been home long when she suffered a fall and broke three ribs. The pain from that was worse than from the operation. She lived alone, and now it was hard to take care of herself. Friends and family helped out.

One night, her mind was full of troubles as she crawled into bed. She felt strange with part of her missing. She felt sorry for herself. There were problems besides the mending of her body. She prayed and asked for guidance.

Juliet turned out the bedside light. In the darkness, tiny sparks of light flashed. She'd experienced them many times before, and had intuited them to be the presences of angels.

Then she noticed a strange light shining over her bed. There was the angel, sparkling away in a soft radiance of light. Only the angel was lit.

Juliet got up and checked to make sure that she hadn't left a light on elsewhere in the house that might be casting an odd angle to light up the angel. Nothing was on. She returned to bed. The little trumpeting angel glittered and glowed in its own mysterious light for several minutes, and then winked out.

Juliet felt much calmer. Her mind was stilled, and peace settled over her like a warm blanket. A message of glad tidings came to her in her thoughts: *You are being taken care of, and all will be well.* All her worry and depression vanished. Juliet drifted off to sleep.

In the months that followed, Juliet regained her strength and her busy calendar. There was no sign of cancer. She thought often of angels, and of the heavenly sign that all in her life would be well. The glowing angel had been a turning point, a release of a great weight of worry and anxiety. And though it never glowed again, it didn't need to, for Juliet knew that she was loved and guided by a higher power that is timeless and eternal.

The
Miracle
of the Light
and the Life

Chris Woodward had just completed his first semester of college at Pennsylvania State University, his first experience of living away from home. Now he was home to share the Christmas break with his parents, Linda and Gary, his younger brother, Aaron, and close relatives. It was a time for family traditions. No one had any inkling that the traditions were about to change forever.

Chris was a quiet young man, a gifted student, quick of mind. He had decided to major in computer science. Though a bit shy around people he didn't know, he enjoyed being with close friends and family, and loved a good joke or a prank. At age eighteen, just entering college, he stood on the threshold of tremendous potential. The world lay before him, ready to be experienced and conquered. Linda and Gary had delivered him to Penn State, sad to see him leave the home nest, but proud to see him initiate his independence. In two more years, Aaron would follow suit.

Gary and Linda hailed from Buffalo, New York, and that year, they and their sons drove from Pennsylvania to Buffalo to spend Christmas with relatives. This year was like the others before it: lots of food, holiday cheer, and good times. But after their return home, Chris suddenly was plagued with debilitating headaches. The headaches persisted and became increasingly severe, accompanied by nausea. Alarmed, Linda attempted to get him into a doctor's office. It was New Year's weekend, and the best she could get was an appointment for the first working day after New Year's Day.

Before they could keep the appointment, Chris abruptly became incoherent and couldn't recognize his surroundings. He didn't know where he was. He wasn't making sense. The Woodwards immediately whisked him off to a hospital emergency room, where he was stabilized. Back home, the headaches and nausea did not relent. The next day, they sought additional medical help.

A terrible truth began to unfold during the next few days. Tests revealed that Chris had an enormous tumor in his brain, located on his rear left side between the parietal and occipital lobes. It was a very aggressive and malignant tumor. The doctor referred them to a neurosurgeon. Although the prognosis was not stated at the time, the level of fear and concern for Chris was very high.

At that moment, the universe imploded. Gary and Linda faced the unthinkable, the worst fear of every parent—the possible loss of their beloved child.

The shock was staggering. They hugged Chris and cried. They vowed to fight the cancer, to beat it in spite of the odds. "I believe in miracles," Linda affirmed. "Miracles happen every day." Indeed, they'd already had one small miracle in the form of Chris's episode of incoherence occurring in the safety of his home. If it had occurred later, after he returned to college, he might have walked into traffic or been in an accident.

The tumor, they learned, may have been growing inside Chris's brain for years before it caused any symptoms. That can sometimes be the case with brain tumors. Depending on their location, they can remain unnoticed for a long time, meanwhile growing to substantial size. When they finally do cause symptoms, they can be difficult to treat. Experts estimated that Chris's remaining life expectancy—which weeks earlier could have been measured by decades—was now only eleven months.

Chris was informed about the nature of his tumor and the treatment necessary for it, but was not told immediately that his cancer was expected to be fatal. The Woodwards saw no reason to destroy his hope, which he would need during the stressful treatment. But if he should ask at any time, he would be told.

With college out of the question, Chris moved back home and began his medical treatment. He weathered the chemotherapy and radiation with a calmness that amazed his parents and was a source of strength for them as well. He took each day as it came.

Gary, an engineer, and Linda, a medical social worker, educated themselves as quickly as possible about Chris's deadly disease and all the options they could pursue. Prayer was an important part of the picture, and Linda contacted numerous prayer lines and services. They participated in a nightly prayer and silent time that linked them to others praying around the world, seeking to fill themselves with the Presence and become channels for healing. They had the support of family and close friends like David and Barbara, who had lost their teenage daughter, Mindy, in a car accident a few years earlier.

Chris rallied under the initial treatment. Gary and Linda poured their energy into fighting the cancer. They were unfamiliar with the field of complementary and alternative therapies, but they wanted to leave no stone unturned. Now they became experts, studying and reading, making calls and investigating. They took Chris to healing services that were a laying on of hands. Linda, led by motherly instinct, continued the laying on of hands at home. They investigated and tried herbs, vitamins, anti-neoplastins, visualizations... *anything* that might work the great miracle of curing Chris.

But Chris's improvement lasted only a few months. By fall, it was apparent that he was deteriorating. The cancer was winning.

Gary and Linda had to face the last thing they ever wanted to confront: that Chris's path was not to survive, but to make his transition into the next world. They had to accept this and let him go. With great pain, they realized that the best thing they could do was to help make his transition as peaceful and as beautiful as possible.

The Arrival of the Invisibles

It was early in November, and Chris was suffering a great deal of pain, despite medication. He was weak and bedridden. Gary and Linda had made him as comfortable as possible in his room. They had already adjusted their work schedules after the initial diagnosis so that at least one of them was with him twenty-four hours a day.

The headaches were unbearable. "I want to die," he told his parents.

Gary and Linda observed a gradual shift in Chris. It was as though he slipped into another state of consciousness. He seemed to float above the pain and was calmer, even blissful. He slept more and lay still more. He seemed more childlike. The Woodwards were informed that the end was near, probably within two to three weeks. They stopped treatments except for pain relief.

When Chris was awake, his awareness now took in the invisible. His eyes would focus in different parts of the room, and he would nod, shake his head, and make facial expressions, as though he were carrying on silent conversations with unseen visitors. An aura of comfort stole over him.

"What do you see?" asked Linda.

Chris struggled to answer, having difficulty finding the right words. His expressive ability was affected by the cancer, but his receptive abilities remained intact. At last he blurted out, "Smidgens!"

"Smidgens?" asked Linda, puzzled.

"Can't you see them? They're *smidgens*—they're all over!"

Linda immediately had a mental picture of cherub angels. What they had read was true—visitors from the next world do come to help prepare the dying. And now Chris was being visited by the heavenly agents of God.

Every day, several times a day, the smidgens called on Chris. It was always evident when they arrived, and they engrossed Chris in a communication only he could perceive. "Can't you see them?" Chris would ask repeatedly of his parents. But the smidgens remained invisible to Gary and Linda and others.

"Some people can see them," Linda told Chris, referring to persons who have clairvoyant abilities. "You're blessed with seeing with spiritual eyes and hearing with spiritual ears. It's so you know where you'll be going."

The smidgens always brought peace and calm to Chris. The angelic support and help were a tremendous solace to Gary and Linda. Chris would not leave this world and go into uncertainty. He was being guided, helped, and prepared by loving ministers of light.

One afternoon a new set of invisible visitors appeared. Linda was keeping Chris company when she observed him take on a focused look that meant he was communicating with presences. She waited until it was apparent that the visitors had left.

Chris wore an uncertain and confused expression. In faltering speech, he told her that there had been several people in the room. "Didn't you see them? They were talking to me. They told me their names. Mostly Woodwards. There was a man with glasses with a different name—I can't remember."

People, thought Linda. *He must be seeing relatives who have died.* She was able to accept this development and discuss it matter-of-factly with Chris. "Could the name have been Fick?" she asked. Fick was her maiden name.

"Yes, that's it," said Chris.

"What did they look like and what did they say?"

Gradually, Linda learned that Chris had seen three women who were short and older, with accents. The man with the glasses did most of the talking—he was the "ringleader," according to Chris.

The descriptions matched deceased relatives whom Chris had not known. Linda's father, George Fick, had died two months after Chris was born. Chris had never met Gary's grandmother and two aunts, Daisy and Dolly, all little Englishwomen. They were dead, too.

Chris pointed to a bulletin board on the wall opposite the bed, which was filled with get-well cards. He relayed that the man with the glasses walked to the board, pointed to a card, and said, "I know this woman. I love her."

Linda brought the bulletin board to Chris's bedside. He pointed to a card with a cat on it. "This is the one," he said. The card was from Linda's mother, Allene.

Linda and Gary got out their wedding albums with photos of Linda's father and Gary's grandmother and aunts. Shown the photos, Chris said, "Yes, this looks like the man and the others."

He was accustomed to the smidgens, but he was confused at the appearance of these unfamiliar people. Linda told him, "Chris, these are relatives that you have never met that have come to tell you about the next life."

He brightened and nodded. "Okay."

What passed between Chris and his visitors remained largely a private matter with Chris. Once, he made his parents laugh heartily when he folded his arms across his chest and announced cockily, "Over there I can have pizza whenever I want!" This was an especially important discovery, as the chemotherapy had required the elimination of cheese from Chris's diet. Linda found it odd to associate pizza with heaven—it certainly wasn't part of her traditional religious upbringing!

On another occasion, she felt confused herself by Chris's experiences, and asked him, "Where do these people say they come from?"

Chris made an effort to find and say the words he wanted. "Life... They say they come from Life."

From Life. To Linda, it was an exquisitely beautiful and hope-giving description. The realm of the dead really was one of Life—of Life Eternal, of life far more glorious than the living can comprehend.

Chris's otherworldly experiences prompted Gary and Linda to begin new areas of study: conscious dying, near-death experiences, and after-death communications. They learned about making closure with the dying, the importance of giving permission to die, and how to help death come as gracefully and with as much dignity as possible. They learned that the dying often begin to experience the next world before they have fully left this one: They have visions of the afterlife, out-of-body trips to the next world, and visitors from the other side. These are real experiences, very important to the dying, and should not be ignored or denied as imagination or hallucinations.

They discussed dying with him, acknowledging that this was soon ahead of him, talking about what it would be like on the other side. They read from inspirational books to him, stories about going toward the light, of being with loved ones again, of going home to God. They began a life review with him, talking about his experiences, things they had done together, and fond memories, all of which provided opportunities for Chris to express his feelings. They played meditation tapes especially for the dying. They were determined that if Chris had to die, he would have a beautiful transition.

The otherworldly aspects of dying seemed strange to Gary and Linda—until a series of highly charged spiritual, even mystical experiences renewed their strength and their faith in divine purpose and presence.

Preparing to Leave

As the days passed and Chris weakened, he slept more. When awake, he seemed to spend more and more time in a different state of consciousness, as though he were already withdrawing from the physical world and becoming oriented to the realm of spirit. The smidgens and the dead were with him daily. The Woodwards could tell by Chris's mannerisms which group was present at a particular time. The smidgens seemed to be all around the room or up near the ceiling. When they came, Chris was infused with a blissful radiance of love. The deceased relatives seemed to cluster around his bed, as though they sat in the chairs and talked to him. He seemed to be very comforted by them.

Chris relayed that he was busy traveling to places unseen and learning about the next world. He saw colors that were so beautiful as to be beyond description. As Linda and Gary learned more about near-death experiences, they were amazed at how his journeys matched the accounts of near-death experiencers. Chris could not articulate all that he saw and learned; Gary and Linda wisely surmised that much of it was not meant for the eyes and ears of the living, but only for those who were about to make their transition.

He began to give indications of being ready to go. He would look at his watch and say, "I have an appointment. What time is my appointment?"

Chris never expressed fear at the prospect of dying. He let them know that he accepted what lay ahead of him. He had questions. "Who will I live with?" he asked Linda.

"You can live with my dad or whatever works out in God's way," she answered.

One day near the end, Linda found tears in Chris's eyes. His speech was especially difficult. She said gently, "Are you worried or concerned about where you're going to go?"

He shook his head. "No."

"Is it that you don't want to leave us?"

Chris nodded. "Yes."

Linda reassured him that it was okay for him to go, that they would miss him physically, but they knew that he would always be close to them. "You're going to be a magnificent spiritual being, Chris. You're going to leave your physical problems here. You will have the ability to think where you want to be and be there. You'll be able to check in on us and know what we're doing and how we are. We're the ones in the dullness here, who will have to work to be aware of you. But we will be able to communicate."

They discussed communicating after death with him, and gave him code words that they would recognize. But Chris would not use words. Instead, he chose light.

The Sign of the Light

The first experience with light happened during the last two weeks of Chris's life. It was early in December, and the Woodwards had put up Christmas decorations early for Chris. His room was full of holiday color, and there were electric candlestick lamps in each of his two windows.

Although Linda was greatly comforted by the spiritual help that Chris was receiving, she wanted to be given some additional tangible signs herself. She dearly wanted a glimpse of her father or of the smidgen angels. She prayed to God and the angels that were with Chris, "If it is in accordance with divine will, please make your presence known to me."

Linda set that intention for a day. The next morning when she entered Chris's room, she could see from his eyes that he was engrossed with his invisible visitors. Not wanting to disturb him, she turned to tiptoe out. Then she noticed that one of the candlestick lamps in the window by the far side of his bed was lit. The light emanating from it seemed unusually bright. Gary and Linda both had slept in Chris's room, and at first Linda thought perhaps they had forgotten to turn it off the night before. Immediately she knew that didn't make sense, for they would have noticed it during the night when they had to attend every few hours to Chris's care and medication. She decided the bulb was probably loose.

Not wanting to disturb Chris's visit with the invisibles, Linda left the room, thinking she would unplug the lamp when she returned. A short time later, she reentered the bedroom. The candlestick lamp was not on. As she rounded the bed to unplug the light, she halted in her tracks and took in her breath. The light was not plugged in to the wall outlet. She stood there, frozen. Chris had been bedbound for weeks now and couldn't have gotten up. And no one had been in the room during her absence—she and Chris were the only ones home. The light had been shining when no electricity could have reached it.

Their presence has been made known, she realized in a rush of gratitude and amazement. *How symbolic to use light.*

Linda thought of their friends, David and Barbara, and their deceased daughter, Mindy. Mindy, who had also visited with Chris along with his dead relatives, communicated with her parents through lights. Perhaps this was a sign that Chris would, too.

By mid-December, the end was at hand. Chris had stayed for about five weeks in his final phase, nearly twice as long as had been expected. Linda knew the extra time had been provided for all of them to make their preparations. Those preparations were done, and now Chris was ready to go. She knew that he would select the moment of his transition.

The Passing

Chris's transition began December 12. He developed a fever and slept most of the day. Even when his eyes were open, it was apparent that he was out of his body. In the evening, after the Woodwards had finished their dinner, he began "primitive breathing," a shallow panting that indicated that his brain and body were shutting down. He slipped from sleep into a coma, and, with his parents beside him, softly breathed his last shortly after midnight. In the space of a breath, beautiful Chris took flight with the angels who were his comfort and his guides.

Linda and Gary sat for a while in silence, feeling his departure, sending him their love, knowing he was going into the Light and into the Life. He was free of the body that no longer served him. A sense of profound peace settled over them. Linda had a vision of Chris soaring, clouds clearing, and a figure in the background, as though she could see through his eyes.

His life in the body was over, but his life in the spirit—and the miracle of the lights—was just beginning.

The Miracle of the Lights

Over the next two days the family held a viewing. Though their grief was beyond words, Gary and Linda were sustained by the energy of participating in Chris's transition. The energy enabled them to minister to grieving family members and friends who arrived from Buffalo.

On the first morning of viewing, their friend David arrived with food for the family and guests who were staying at the house. The day was dark, rainy and gloomy, adding to the sadness shared by all. David stepped into the foyer; the overhead lights were on to chase away the grayness of the day.

"You were so blessed to witness what Chris went through," he comforted Linda. "It's helped us a lot, and it will help others, too."

Linda nodded. "I know we were blessed. But you know, David, when someone you love dies, no matter how firmly you believe in an afterlife, that belief is put to the test. You need to know beyond a shadow of a doubt that life goes on forever and ever, and that there really is so much help on the other side. I need that one last confirmation, the 'Hey, Mom, I'm fine.'"

The words were barely out of her mouth when the light above them blinked off and on. David and Linda both looked up. David chuckled. "There's your answer!"

The light demonstration—their first after-death communication—buoyed their spirits, validating for them that not only was Chris all right, he was present with them as well.

Linda silently prayed to the angels to help her and Gary ease the grief felt by their relatives. "Please, if you could do something dramatic with lights to help comfort our family?" she asked. "It would be wonderful."

The response was not long in coming—although they did not recognize it at first. The next evening, after the viewing ended, Gary and Linda were driving a minivan full of family members back home, which was but a few minutes away by car. The stretch van was only a year old; Gary had purchased it early that year for meeting Chris's transportation needs to and from the hospital. The van had two sets of reading lights on the ceiling, two over the front seats and two over the second row of passenger seats. They came on automatically when the doors were opened, and went off when the doors were closed. Anyone could turn on an individual light by reaching up and pushing a button on the ceiling console. A loud click would be heard.

After everyone got in the van and the doors were closed, Gary noticed that one of the rear lights was on. He thought perhaps somebody bumped the console, although it would have required an unusual maneuver. He turned it off. It didn't occur to Gary or Linda that the light was no accident, until the following day.

Chris's funeral was scheduled for the morning. After breakfast, the family went to the funeral parlor. During the short ride in the van, they again noticed that one of the back lights was on again, seemingly by itself. Suddenly the meaning of it became clear. Excited, Gary and Linda shared their thoughts about what was happening, that Chris was communicating with them through lights. The family shared their enthusiasm, albeit with a touch of skepticism.

Following the casket-closing ceremony, a procession of guests drove to the church where the funeral service would take place. Once again in the Woodwards' van, a rear light mysteriously was on. Chris was there, riding with them, participating in his own funeral. The sign from beyond gave their spirits a great boost, and helped them through the difficult day.

On the way from the church to the mausoleum, nothing unusual happened. Perhaps it was due to everyone staring intently at the lights. But on the way home, a rear light once again winked on. Even Gary's skeptical father, Frank, acknowledged, "Nobody was *near* that light."

In less than twenty-four hours, during four out of five trips in the van, a rear light had come on for no apparent reason. It was never the same light, but either of two rear lights. The Woodwards had experienced no prior problems with the lights in the year that they had owned the van. An examination of the van determined that it would be nearly impossible for a person to turn the light on accidentally. It would require a bump of the head on the ceiling console while leaning forward toward the front seats. And, there would be that audible click of the switch.

The lights were nothing short of a miracle for Gary and Linda, bridging the fathomless distance between the worlds.

After Chris's interment on December 15, there were no more light episodes until Christmas.

Gary, Linda, and Aaron drove up to Buffalo for the traditional family get-together. The holiday weighed heavily upon them; they were feeling Chris's absence acutely. It would be all they could do to get through Christmas.

On Christmas Eve, the Woodwards went to church with Gary's parents, Frank and Doris. Gary drove the family in the van. After church, they went to the home of one of Gary's sisters, Terry. Linda and Gary and Gary's parents then got into the van to return to Frank and Doris's home. On the way, the conversation turned to the pies Doris had baked, and the kinds the boys liked—Chris had been especially fond of lemon meringue. At the mention of his favorite pie, they realized that a rear light in the van was on. Doris looked up and smiled. "He's with us again." Chris, ever fond of a family joke, was giving them a wink.

The Woodwards stayed with Gary's parents. On Christmas morning, everyone piled in the van to travel to the home of Gary's other sister, Gerry, for the festivities of gift opening. A rear light was on again. It was just the tonic they needed to stay in good spirits throughout the day.

Light and Life Everlasting

Chris continued to make his presence known through lights. Months would go by without a sign, then he would show up at a moment when he was most needed. Like the following February, on a bleak night when Gary had just finished a marathon stretch at work. He was tired and hungry, and in deep pain over the loss of Chris. Two months had gone by, and he missed him intensely. Gary climbed into the cold van and started the engine. He was about to drive off when he noticed that a rear light was on. He had been the only person in the van that day. He grinned and the burden of his loneliness lifted. Chris was coming through to comfort him.

When time came for the Woodwards to take Aaron to college for his first semester, Chris was there, too. It was a bittersweet feeling to leave Aaron at his dormitory. They were happy for Aaron, but were reminded of the time they had brought Chris for his first and only semester of college. On the way off the campus, Linda spoke aloud. "Chris, I know you're here. Please stay with Aaron and make sure he's all right." She'd barely said the words when she noticed that a rear light was on.

Chris's passing and the spiritual experiences surrounding it led Linda to open her ability as an energy healer. She often feels Chris's presence when she works. She knows from her prayer and meditation that he has chosen to help others still on the earth plane.

Gary and Linda have turned their sorrow into help for others as well. They are active in Compassionate Friends, a support group for parents who have lost children.

In the beginning, Linda had prayed for a miracle. Prayers are answered and miracles happen, sometimes not as we wish, but in accordance with a divine plan too great for us to comprehend. Chris's miracle is the miracle of the Light and the Life, which are eternal, and of love, which never ends.

The
Angelic
Mechanic

Christmas was about two weeks away. For most of the day on this brisk Saturday, eighteen-year-old Rick[*] and several of his young friends from church had worked at a community food collection center, helping to sort the charity donations that were to be sent to families in need. It was rewarding work; it felt good to be doing something to help others. The collection center operated year-round, but at Christmastime the donations poured in, and extra volunteer help was always needed.

Late in the afternoon, Rick finished his last task and collected his friends: Jim, April, Beth, and Gwen. They had a long drive ahead of them, and Rick, who provided the transportation, had promised everyone that they would be at their homes for dinner.

---

[*] *All names have been changed.*

The three girls sat in the back. Jim took the passenger front seat. The girls chatted and gossiped among themselves; Jim and Rick traded sports small talk.

Rick opted for country back roads instead of the highway. There wasn't much traffic on the back roads. Few were marked with road signs, but he knew a few shortcuts.

They were about halfway home when the old Ford started acting up. The trouble began with misfires in the engine. With every resounding pop, the car shook. It didn't sound or feel good. Rick grimaced and wondered what was up. His car wasn't in the greatest shape, but it should be roadworthy.

The car misfired again with an enormous bang and this time Rick felt a loss of power in the engine. The car began slowing, despite the fact that Rick kept his foot on the accelerator.

"Better see what's the matter," he muttered, and pulled the car off to the side of the road. The engine stalled before he brought the car to a halt. After braking to a stop, Rick tried to restart the car. The engine cranked over and over without catching.

They all got out. The air was crisp and chilly. "Great wheels," teased Beth.

Rick shrugged and raised the hood of the car. He and Jim peered down into the interior. Neither one of them was much of a mechanic, but they were too embarrassed to admit that to the girls. Weren't guys all supposed to be wizards with cars?

Much of the guts of the car looked foreign to them. They poked here and there halfheartedly and made a stab at appearing to know what they were doing. Rick got back in the driver's seat and tried to start the car again. It refused to respond.

He glanced into the sky. The sun was low in the west, metamorphosing into an orange-red ball. It would be dark soon. The countryside around them was rolling farmland. Fences running alongside the road indicated private property. But there were no houses in sight. This stretch of back roads in the New Jersey countryside wasn't well traveled. It certainly wasn't the place to be stuck—especially on a cold December night.

The girls came around and peered around the boys' shoulders. "What's wrong?" asked Gwen. "Why won't it start?"

Rick and Jim looked at each other. "We don't know," Rick admitted reluctantly.

"What do you mean, you don't know?" demanded April.

"Sorry, girls," said Jim. He smiled sheepishly.

April looked around her and shivered, pulling her jacket closer to her. "So what do we do? Start walking?"

"No way," protested Beth. "We don't know where we are. We could be miles from anyplace. It's nearly dark."

"The guys should go," suggested Gwen.

The girls chorused their approval of the idea.

Rick pushed back from the front of the car and addressed the group. "Look, we don't know how to fix the car, but we all know how to pray. So let's get going and pray about this. We'll each take a turn."

They formed a little circle, held hands, and bowed their heads. One by one, they asked for divine intervention. When Rick's turn came, he prayed, "Father we thank you for the blessings you have given us. Now we're having trouble with our car, Lord. We ask that if it be your will, help restore it to working order so that we can get home safely."

A quiet settled over the five teenagers when they finished praying. They looked around, as if expecting the miracle of a tow truck to appear on the road. But the road was empty, and darkness was gathering.

Rick tried repeatedly without success to start the car. "Let's pray again," he said.

Once more they formed a ring and made their prayers. As they finished, Rick looked up and could scarcely believe his eyes. A man had suddenly appeared on the other side of one fence a short way down the road. He jumped over the fence with athletic ease and came jogging up to the car. He was of indeterminant age but youthful, and was tall with dark hair. Overall, he was a nice-looking man but strangely rather stone-faced.

He neither smiled nor spoke, but went straight to the engine and began poking around. The girls fell back, too astonished to speak.

"Hello, sir," Rick ventured. The man did not reply. In a stammering voice, Rick attempted to explain what had happened, but the man did not appear interested in what he had to say. It seemed that he was on a single-minded mission to fix the car. He pulled and pushed various things and grunted. Rick looked at him while he worked. His clothes looked freshly cleaned and pressed. The man didn't seem concerned about the possibility of getting them dirty.

The teenagers stood in uncertain silence while the stranger worked. After a short while, the man straightened up. Rick noticed, even in the gathering gloom, that his eyes were the bluest he had ever seen.

"Try it," the man barked.

Rick scurried to slide behind the wheel. When he turned the ignition, the engine flared to life.

"I wouldn't turn it off if I were you," said the mysterious stranger.

Before Rick or any of the others could speak, the man turned and loped back up the road. He vaulted the fence, again effortlessly, and then was gone from sight.

Rick wasted no time slamming the hood shut. "Let's go!"

"Who was *that?*" April wondered as they rolled down the country road.

"Somebody local," offered Gwen. But no one, not even Gwen, really thought that somehow a local person had just appeared out of nowhere to fix their car.

"We asked God for help," said Rick. Then he blurted, "Maybe he sent us an angel."

"That guy was *real,*" said Beth. The others agreed.

"Well, angels can look like us if they want to," replied Rick, not quite convinced himself. "Remember the three angels who came to visit Abraham, and passed for people."

They debated the reality of angels for a while. If angels were present in ancient times, then surely they were present now. But didn't angelic help have to involve something really important? Would an angel appear to help a group of kids stranded in a car?

Why not?

A quiet settled over the teenagers for the rest of the way home.

For a long time, Rick thought about the incident and the strange man who knew just what to do. He settled on what his heart told him was true: Prayer works, and angels are for real. This would be a Christmas to remember for the rest of his life.

The
Christmas
Visit

The call came at 2:55 A.M. on an October Monday morning. Jackie was roused out of a deep sleep by the ringing telephone. Her mother, Darlene, was on the other end of the line.

Everyone in the family—Jackie and her five siblings, their spouses, and children—knew that Darlene hadn't been feeling well. She had a thyroid condition, but was reluctant to seek medical help. Two days before, Darlene had dropped off some Halloween decorations at one of her daughters' houses, and went home quickly because she didn't feel well. She professed to feel better the next day.

Now she was calling Jackie in the middle of the night. She sounded bright and upbeat. "Can you come over?" she asked.

Jackie was alarmed despite the tone of her mother's voice. "What's the matter? Are you all right?"

"Well, not great," Darlene confessed. "Can you come?"

Darlene lived about thirty minutes from Jackie. Two other daughters were much closer, but for some reason, Darlene specifically wanted Jackie.

"Yes, of course," said Jackie. She jumped out of bed. As she pulled on her clothes, a queer feeling came over her. She told her husband, Mike, where she was going. He shared her concern about Darlene.

The rural Michigan roads were dark but familiar to Jackie. She sped along. At precisely 3:15—she glanced at the dashboard clock's digital face— she was suddenly gripped by panic. *Oh, please, God, let me get there in time,* she found herself praying. *She's going.* Although there was no logical reason to think it, Jackie knew that her mother was dying.

As soon as she made the prayer, a feeling of deep calm settled over Jackie. Her body tingled. The car seemed magically to float over the road as if being driven by unseen hands.

Jackie hurried into her mother's house and found Darlene lying on the couch. She knew she was dead, but tried anyway to rouse her. In shock, Jackie mechanically lifted the telephone receiver and placed a call to the 911 emergency services. She administered cardiopulmonary resuscitation, even though she knew her mother was gone.

Darlene had died swiftly of a ruptured aneurysm that burst in her heart. Her death was a deep and severe blow to the entire family.

Later, when Jackie had time to collect her thoughts, she realized that she had known the instant her mother made her transition—at 3:15 A.M. She felt it was an angel who administered the calm to her, preparing her to face the shock and get through it.

Jackie also intuitively knew that her mother probably sensed that she was about to leave. She had turned to Jackie because, of all the siblings, Jackie could best manage the devastation of finding her mother dead.

Jackie later learned that three of her four sisters had strange experiences the night their mother died. Toni awakened at exactly 3:15 A.M. feeling a breeze gently blowing on her face—a sign, it is said, of the presence of an angel. Two other sisters had unusual difficulty sleeping that night.

In the numb days that followed, plans were made for Darlene's funeral. Jackie felt her mother's presence and "knew" what she wanted at her service. Jackie believed strongly in both life after death and the ability of the dead to communicate with the living. Her father, Robert, had appeared to her and to Darlene several times since his death. So to Jackie it did not seem unusual that her mother should make her presence known, too.

After Darlene's funeral, Jackie struggled to cope with her grief. She prayed for help. She desperately missed her mother, and longed for an explanation as to why she was taken away so suddenly. She knew that Darlene had missed Robert and was ready to go. She would not have wanted to endure a lingering illness or an impaired life. Even though Jackie believed that her mother was in a better place—with God—she wanted more than anything to see her again, and to know for certain that she was all right. She was consumed with thoughts of her mother almost every waking minute. She talked to her mother all the time.

As though in answer to her prayers, angels suddenly entered Jackie's life. The angelic door opened about a month after Darlene's death. Jackie and Mike took a trip to the family lakeside retreat in northern Michigan. In the past, it had been customary for Darlene to come along with them. While Mike hunted deer, Jackie and Darlene would have fun shopping in a nearby town. They would all get together for a festive dinner. Now it was Jackie shopping alone, missing the companionship of her mother.

Without knowing why, she was drawn to a little bookshop, and went immediately to the section that carried books about angels. She felt an odd tingling through her body as she reached for a book about how to talk to your angels. She knew she had to buy it. She stayed up all night long reading it.

The book recommended that a person become quiet and simply ask, "I want to talk to my angels," like a little prayer repeated over and over again until a response came. Jackie tried this, at first without results, perhaps because she was nervous. One day, back at work, she prayed during her lunch hour. This time, she used a Catholic prayer, "Jesus, Mary, and Joseph." She repeated this in a singsong voice out loud. On the third time, she found herself automatically repeating the name Mary as fast as she could. A surge of energy shot through her, bringing the tingling again. Tears spilled down her cheeks as she was lifted into a marvelous ecstasy. She had been touched by an exalted presence: the Blessed Virgin Mary.

Communications came frequently after that. After initiating the way, the Mary presence faded into the background and Darlene came forward. Jackie could hear her mother's voice, not with her inner ear, but as though Darlene were alive and speaking to her. The voice came to her especially when she was alone, such as driving in the car. She consulted a gifted channeler and received additional messages. Darlene told her that she would be staying around for a while at Jackie's house and Toni's house, watching over them like a guardian angel.

Jackie often asked for her mother's help and advice. When she searched for a new job, Darlene accurately indicated which opening would be hers. Darlene also assisted Jackie with gardening and decorations in her home, interests they had both shared. Darlene had lavished much love and attention on her own yard. The now-familiar tingling Jackie felt announced Darlene's presence. Often her melodic voice would follow: "Hello, Jackie. I love you, Jackie." Darlene also appeared in Jackie's dreams, as well as in dreams Jackie shared with Toni. The dreams were intense, realistic encounters.

Despite the communications, it was hard for Jackie to face the first Christmas without her mother. The traditional family gathering at sister Sue's house was planned as usual, but Jackie knew that their mother's absence would be acutely felt by all.

The family dined on a sumptuous prime rib dinner—a favorite of Darlene's and Robert's—and then relaxed with Christmas music, television, cards, and games.

It was late by the time Jackie and Mike left to drive home. Exhausted, Jackie looked forward to climbing into bed. Despite the holiday gaiety, she felt despondent, missing her mother.

Jackie and Mike arrived at their house around midnight, parked the car in the garage, and entered through the kitchen. Jackie glanced up into the dining room and could not believe her eyes. There stood her mother, looking as real as she had in life. She was fresh, youthful, and happy, and was dressed in one of her favorite outfits, blue slacks and a vibrant floral blouse. She was leaning casually against the dining room table, one elbow propped on the table, her legs crossed at the ankles. A purse hung from one shoulder. She was smiling at Jackie.

Jackie stopped short. Mike, behind her, nearly bumped into her. "What are you looking at?" he asked, bewildered.

The magical moment was broken and Darlene vanished.

"I just saw Mom!" said Jackie, astonished.

Mike smiled. "I'm not surprised. Christmas was your mother's favorite holiday."

Jackie was aglow. She had wanted to see her mother again, but never really expected it to happen. But it did—there was no doubt about it. Much more than her voice and the dreams, the appearance of Darlene was proof to Jackie that she really was watching over the family. It was so wonderful!

Darlene's visit changed Jackie's life, and the lives of her family. She shared with them what had happened to her. In the months that followed, other members of her family had some miraculous experiences of their own with Darlene. Once Toni saw her in the middle of the night. She got up, and on her way back to bed, suddenly saw Darlene before her. Darlene came to Toni and brushed her cheek against her. She gave Toni a big hug, one she could feel. "I love you, Toni," her mother said, and disappeared.

Darlene's guardian angel presence brought tremendous comfort to all in the family. That Christmas visit opened up Jackie's mind and heart even more to the realm of angels, and to learn all she could about them. She became aware of other angelic presences around her as well.

Jackie still missed her mother—she knew she probably always would. But she rejoiced in thanks and gratitude for the gifts that Darlene brought her about angels, everlasting life, God, and love.

Choices
and
Consequences

Janie was awestruck at the rugged, mystical beauty of Crete. This was the land where Zeus was born, and the whispers of the gods echoed in the ancient mountains and rode the crystal blue waves of the Mediterranean Sea. Janie had come to Crete to find inner healing. To recharge her soul. It was the beginning of April, just after Easter. A fitting time to recenter and find rebirth.

Janie was a singer. Always had been. From a very young age, she had known that her clear and vibrant voice was a gift from God. Growing up in poverty, it was about the only possession she could call hers. One Christmas Eve when she was about fifteen years old, she was left alone for a while in front of a big store window. As she gazed into the window, she remembered a Christmas story about a clown who had no gift, so he performed for God as the only gift he had. She thought about that story and then said a prayer,

Jesus, I don't have anything to offer you, but like the clown I will give you the only gift I have to give you and that is to perform a song for you. And with that, Janie sang the most beautiful song she knew.

Since that day, whenever Janie practiced her singing, she sang two songs to God in thankfulness for the gift of her voice. "The More I See You" and "Through the Eyes of Love" were her love songs to God. Sometimes she could hardly get through them without breaking down into tears.

The pressures on Janie had been many over the years. She'd had to cope with alcoholism in the family. She had suffered from extreme anxiety attacks from her teens to age forty. There was abuse during a failed marriage. After her children were born, she started to drink, not excessively, but a bit too much, she often thought.

Now she was happily remarried, but there was still a lot of inner healing to do. And so Janie had come to Crete, drawn by a conference on "healing the wounded healer" and by the exotic lure of Crete itself. The setting for the conference was spectacular: a resort hotel literally carved out of a hillside, its huge, colonnaded marble structure seeming like the very temple of the gods. The weather was chilly and the sea was wild.

On her first night, Janie had an amazing dream. It was a dream so sharp and vivid that she had no doubt that it was real.

A host of angels descended from the sky. They looked very human. Each angel was assigned to a person attending the conference. The angels arrived carrying Christmas decorations. Janie thought that was strange, because she knew it was April. She didn't know the significance of that, but she laughed because she didn't particularly like Christmas, due to unhappy memories of it as a child. She never decorated for it or celebrated it.

Janie suddenly found herself in a grocery store. The angel assigned to her, a woman, was working behind the counter. Janie approached the counter carrying a bottle of vodka. She saw that she had forgotten chips, so she went to find them and bought a bag back to the counter. At first she felt strange and ashamed to have her angel see that she had vodka. But the angel was not judgmental and took her money with a big smile.

Then all the angels left, taking the Christmas decorations with them.

The dream had a profound effect on Janie. It made her realize that there really were higher forces who noticed her and what she was doing with herself. She realized that even though her angel lovingly took her money for her purchase of liquor, the unspoken message was, *It's your choice, but you will pay the price.* We aren't judged for what we do; but whatever we do carries a consequence. Janie knew she had to take control of her habit instead of letting it control her.

The Christmas decorations in the dream carried multiple symbolisms. One was the childhood roots of anxiety, which can lead to false solutions like alcohol. Another symbol of the decorations was celebration. Healing is always cause for celebration. Yet another symbolism was rebirth. Easter stands for rebirth, but so does Christmas. Christmas represents a rebirth of hope, optimism, and love.

Janie went home from Crete healed, a new song in her heart.

A Brush
of Angel Wings

t was nearly 5 P.M. on Christmas Eve, and Jack was in a bit of a hurry. He'd just gotten off work, and was due to meet his parents and a sister at his aunt Ann's house for the traditional holiday get-together.

Jack got onto the freeway and moved into the fast lane. The road was clean and dry. He came up behind a car traveling much slower. Thinking that the driver was not going to move over to let him pass, he swung to the right to pass in the middle lane. Just at the same moment, the driver of the car in front of him also moved into the middle lane. Jack swerved sharply back into the fast lane, but not enough to avoid clipping the car as he passed it. The impact was enough to send both cars spinning out of control.

Jack's car bounced off the side barrier, careened across the freeway like a pinball, and hit the other side barrier. He wasn't wearing his seat belt, and his face and head took the brunt of the impacts. Everything went black.

Fortunately, a trauma center was about two miles away, and emergency medical crews were quick to arrive at the scene of the accident. They found Jack outside of his crumpled car, unconscious, with severe head wounds. They rushed him to the trauma center. His belongings were handed over to a state trooper—the customary procedure for traffic fatalities. Apparently, Jack, twenty-four, was not expected to survive. The two occupants of the other car were much luckier, with lesser injuries.

Back at Ann's house, Jean wondered what had happened to her son. She wasn't too worried—she figured that perhaps he had gotten home tired and had decided to stay put rather than come to dinner. All three of the Reistle children still lived at home: Jack and his sisters, Jill and Joy. Jill was baby-sitting; Joy had come to dinner at Ann's. Well, thought Jean, there would be tomorrow, Christmas Day, when the family would gather at her brother Jerry's house. Jack could join them then.

The evening ended without Jack. Jean, her husband, John, and Joy bade good-bye and returned home. When they pulled into their driveway and saw that Jack's car was gone, Jean was immediately gripped by panic. "Oh, my God, what's happened?" she said. "Where's Jack?"

They went into the house. Jean let the dogs out. She felt uneasy. It wasn't right for Jack to be gone. He hadn't come to dinner, and now there was no note of explanation for his absence. Jean wondered what to do, whom to call. Her questions were answered within minutes when the headlights of a car showed, coming down the long lane to their house. It was a police car.

John went outside. A short time later he came back inside the house, shaken. "Jack's been in an accident," he said grimly, and related what the police had told him.

Jean went into shock. She imagined the worst—that Jack would die or was already dead. The twenty-minute ride to the trauma center seemed interminable, with terrible fears crowding her mind. She remained silent, and so did John and Joy. Jean's anxiety escalated when they arrived at the trauma center and were ushered into the "family room." If Jack were alive, she worried, wouldn't they have taken them to see him without delay? The minutes mounted and no one came to talk to them. They sat for what seemed an eternity. *He's gone, he's gone,* Jean cried to herself.

Finally John went out into the hall and corralled an employee. "Can't somebody tell us *something?*" he pleaded.

With apologies, the Reistles were taken to the ward where the most serious trauma patients were kept. Jean's worst fear was dispelled when a nurse told them that Jack was alive and they were still trying to get him stabilized. The family could see him in a few minutes. "Don't be alarmed by the way he looks," the nurse cautioned, explaining that they hadn't yet cleaned up all the blood. Jean didn't care—the thing that mattered the most was that her son was alive.

Jack, still unconscious, was covered with cuts, bruises, and scratches. His nose was broken. One eye was so horribly swollen that Jean feared he would never see out of it again. A web of tubes connected him to an array of machines.

But there was more cautionary news. A doctor explained that Jack had suffered brain injuries that probably would affect three functions: memory, personality, and mathematical ability. Time would tell the extent of the injuries, and how much those three functions would change.

The hardest for Jean to imagine was personality. Did that mean that Jack would no longer be Jack? It was impossible to contemplate.

Jean urged John and Joy to go home and get some rest. She knew sleep would be impossible for her—she would spend the night at the hospital, keeping a vigil in the waiting room. Doctors urged her to go home, too, but she shook her head.

The atmosphere of the waiting room was cold and sterile. Jean resolved to stay awake, fearful that she might fall asleep and not be found if an emergency occurred during the night. She positioned herself so that she could watch the door. She still was filled with dread that Jack would not be able to hang on to his life. It was almost as if her staying awake would keep death away.

The hands of the clock on the wall moved in slow motion. Every minute was an hour. Shortly after 11 P.M., Jean was witness to the most devastating news a family ever could hear. A doctor informed several members of a family that their son had just died. Crushed and tearful, they joined hands in a little circle and prayed for him. Jean's heart went out to them. How unbearably sad, especially on Christmas Eve. She huddled into her chair, thinking, *When is it going to be my turn? The doctor will come for me.*

But no doctor came to Jean with the news she dreaded, and the night passed without further incident. Dawn pushed away grim shadows, bringing rays of light and hope.

John, Joy, and Jill arrived around eight on Christmas morning and joined Jean's vigil, waiting for visiting hours to begin at eleven. Soon another visitor arrived—Sandy, the Methodist minister for whom Jean worked as a secretary. John had called her the previous evening to notify her of Jack's accident, and now she was taking time from her own family holiday activities to be with the Reistles. They all went in to see Jack together.

Jack had the only private room in the ward. They gathered around his bed and talked. He was in a coma. The equipment monitoring him beeped and flashed.

Sandy asked, "Would you like me to say a prayer?"

"Yes," said Jean gratefully.

They held hands in a ring around his bed, one of them placing a hand on Jack to make him part of the ring. Sandy began to pray. The words were a soothing balm.

As Jean listened, she suddenly felt herself flooded with an indescribable warmth. It came down on her shoulders like a mantle of fleece from heaven. She had never felt anything so special, so unusual. It was like two wings coming down to wrap around her shoulders. The entire room was suffused with peace and comfort. Jean wondered if the warmth was the presence of

God. *No, not on Christmas,* she thought immediately. *He's much too busy today!* Then she wondered if the presence were her deceased mother and father, coming to her to reassure her that all would be well with Jack. Whatever the presence was, it brought her peace with whatever would be the outcome.

Jack regained consciousness on December 30. He came awake shocked to find himself injured and lying in a hospital bed; he had no idea what had happened to him. He did not remember the accident.

On New Year's Day, Jack went home. He was wobbly and still concussed, and very sensitive to noises. Upon his return, his family celebrated a delayed Christmas.

Within two weeks, Jack was back at work. Jean drove him. Over the next several months, he quickly and miraculously healed of his injuries, including the trauma to his brain. His personality remained unchanged. His ability in math was still as good as ever. He was at times a trifle more forgetful. He regained his health and married his girlfriend, Jen, who had stood by him during his recovery.

As for Jean, she developed a sudden, inexplicable interest in angels. She had never thought much about them, but now she began collecting them and reading about them. She couldn't get enough of angels. It was almost an obsession. Then the realization came to her: The winged presence in Jack's trauma room was an angel—Jean's guardian angel, come to bring her comfort and peace. It was a healing presence, and Jack had been healed back into a full and productive life.

Jean still thanks God and her guardian angel every day for the gift of Jack's life and recovery. She gives thanks for the awareness of angels coming into her life. She also gives thanks for another gift: her first grandchild, a cute-as-a-button little girl, Leah, born to Jack and Jen.

Christmas Eve no longer has the stain of tragedy upon it, but remains a happy family time. Jean often thinks of that Christmas morning when she felt the angel's wings, a sign that God is aware of each and every soul under his care.

The Heart-Shaped Stone

$\mathcal{A}$s marriages go, the union between Charlotte and Bob Abell was strong and long. Like all marriages, it had its ups and downs, times of closeness and times of distance. But they loved and were in love, and the love nurtured between them was deep.

In the months before their thirty-fourth wedding anniversary, Bob seemed to grow more introspective than usual. He had enjoyed a full career as a state employee, from trooper all the way to chief investigator. He had taken early retirement. Now he worked at the local racetrack, where he liked being around all the people. He was well loved by those who worked with him. Lately, however, he seemed to have a lot on his mind.

In retrospect, it seemed that those months were more about closure, a tying up of loose ends. If Charlotte had only read the signs. But then again, she thought later, if she had read the signs correctly, she would not have been able to bear the truth of them.

They had talked about old hurts and pains, not only between the two of them, but between Bob and others. They talked about Bob's worries about getting old. He feared a diminished life, and not being able to cope. They talked about what Bob wanted when he died—cremation—and what sort of marker he wanted for his grave. Dying seemed to be remote, in the distant future, to Charlotte. She had no idea that death was just around the corner. But Bob must have known it, on some level of his soul.

The soul searching and time spent together brought Charlotte and Bob much closer than they had been in a long time. They enjoyed a resurgence of passion and intimacy that had graced the early years of their marriage. Charlotte felt as though they were on the threshold of a new beginning, a renaissance of partnership.

The day before Bob died, they enjoyed a leisurely morning, making love after breakfast and then going for a walk in the countryside that surrounded their home. They did some shopping. Their thirty-fourth wedding anniversary was only two days away. It had been their tradition to celebrate their anniversary with a dinner of steamed crabs. "Let's do it tonight," said Bob spontaneously. And so they bought the fixings and some beer, and settled into a romantic dinner at home. They talked and talked.

Charlotte awoke during the night. She found Bob awake, too. He commented that he was having a hard night and felt restless.

The next day, Charlotte went off to a seminar and Bob went off to work. They kissed each other good-bye. Once again, Charlotte was filled with the sense of a new beginning.

Bob never came home. Instead, he was called home to God.

On the way back from the track at the end of his workday, Bob suffered a ruptured aneurysm in his brain, probably killing him instantly. His foot on the gas pedal, the pickup truck raced faster and faster, and went careening off the side of the road. It roared between a fence and a telephone pole, tore across a road—miraculously missing oncoming traffic—and then somehow squeezed between two trees before smashing into a tree that had been cut down. The truck motor immediately burst into flames.

Not far behind Bob in traffic was an off-duty county policeman, who was at the scene of the accident within minutes. He and another witness smashed the truck's window and pulled Bob out. They administered cardio-pulmonary resuscitation, but Bob was already gone. It was 6:52 P.M.

At the seminar, Charlotte talked about Bob, was talking about him at the moment he died. Later, it seemed that she had cleared a path for him.

Charlotte and Bob had not planned to eat dinner together that evening, so after the seminar, Charlotte went out to eat with a friend. But when she arrived home and found the driveway empty, she had a sudden, chilling flash about Bob. She *knew.* She immediately tried to dispel the fear. *No, no, he's just out having a beer, having a good time with the guys,* she tried to convince herself.

A few minutes later, she heard voices outside in the driveway.

Thank God, she thought. *Bob's truck must have broken down and he got a ride.*

Then she saw that the visitors were the police, a chaplain, and Bob's brother, Johnny.

"Where's Bob?" Charlotte asked anxiously, although she knew the dreadful answer.

The men wouldn't say a thing until they had her seated in the house. The shock was still incredible, like the world exploding into bits. Charlotte looked at Johnny. "This is a dream, isn't it—just a dream?"

Johnny shook his head sadly. "No, it's for real."

Charlotte felt as though she snapped back and forth between realities. In one reality was the shock of Bob's death, and the men talking to her about it. In another reality was the world just gone—she and Bob together in a renewed marriage. "Where's Bob now?" Charlotte managed to ask through a haze of tears. "Can I go see him?" But it was late Saturday night, and the morgue was closed until Monday, she was told. Johnny asked her who should be called. Given Bob's wallet by the police officer, Charlotte clutched it to her. It was the only thing of his she had now. She walked about, moaning in her grief. Soon the house filled with grieving relatives.

The next day, instead of celebrating her wedding anniversary, Charlotte was planning her husband's funeral.

The funeral service was held in a clearing in the woods on family land behind Charlotte and Bob's house. Later, Charlotte and her daughter, Melissa, and niece, Mary, took his ashes to scatter in the ocean. At the moment they scattered the ashes, three dolphins appeared. Charlotte knew it was a good sign. Dolphins, a symbol of Christ, are the bearers of souls to the afterlife. And three is the number of the holy trinity, of the ascent of the soul to higher planes.

In the weeks that followed, Charlotte and Melissa drew strength and comfort from angels. Both were attuned to the angelic host through their years of spiritual and metaphysical work. They had long felt the presence of angels around them, and knew that angels were part of God's plan for the world. Now, the angels' inner messages of guidance and support helped to relieve the valleys of grief.

The first Christmas without Bob was hard and empty. Nonetheless, Charlotte made an effort to maintain family traditions. She purchased a beautiful tree and decorated it with lights and ornaments that she and Bob had collected during their years together. The familiar glitter and seasonal joy were comforting, but did not dispel the emptiness and loneliness. She went through the motions of opening gifts with Melissa and her partner, Ernie. The angels had told Melissa to watch for a surprise. When a hawk flew overhead, chased by two crows, they saw it as a sign of Bob's presence. Later, they visited Bob's grave in the woods and did a ritual.

Charlotte was relieved when the holiday season came to a close.

A year went by. Charlotte's sorrow seemed to know no end. She would go through old photo albums and cry, missing the life that no longer was. The second Christmas without Bob, Charlotte couldn't muster the energy to celebrate the holiday. Christmas would never be the same again, and she was much changed over the course of the year. Loneliness covered her like a chill fog, permeating her bones. This year, she decided, there would be no special Christmas tree, fewer gifts, no traditional dinner. Her little Norwegian pine tree, which she'd had for years, served as the Christmas tree. Charlotte deco-rated it with little red bows and a few angels.

While placing the decorations on the little tree, Charlotte had the impression that the tree would enjoy having lights as well. She added two strands of tiny lights. Small and fragile, the tree had all it could do to hold the lights and decorations and remain standing. In a way, it represented how Charlotte felt: small and fragile, bearing a great load, but still standing.

Charlotte added more decorations throughout the house. The bright reds and greens made the winter seem less bleak. She wrapped her gifts and placed them around the little tree.

Christmas Eve arrived. Loneliness pressed in on Charlotte, and time seemed to go by slowly. She felt a nudge from her angels to take a walk in the woods behind the house. She was reluctant to tread upon old memories. It had been one of the greatest joys of Christmas for Charlotte and Bob to walk together in the woods and gather crowfoot to make wreaths and deco-rations for the house. She simply couldn't go out alone this year. To scour the hillsides without the companionship of Bob was asking too much.

However, the idea of taking a walk, but to a different area, persisted. At last Charlotte yielded. *Okay, okay,* she conceded. She pulled on a jacket and went outside to meander in the woods along a deer path. The ground was damp from prior rain, giving the woods a heavy musky smell. Gray clouds covered the sky, depressing her spirits even further.

She trudged along, lost in thoughts of loneliness and wishing for what could no longer be. She took a path down a steep hill. She could not help but think of how she and Bob had cut wood on this very hill, and had walked this path together many times. She hadn't been down it since he died.

Suddenly, Charlotte stumbled over a sizable rock and nearly landed on her face. Strange—she had never noticed such a stone along this way before. Something inside her told her that it was the sign she was seeking.

She retraced her steps and looked at the offending stone. It was an absolutely gorgeous rock, shaped liked a heart! It even had the look of a heart's muscle at the top of it in the form of crystalline globs. White crystal quartz ran from the glob at the top all the way to the bottom. Veins of quartz radiated from the center vein, giving it the look of arteries and veins in the heart. She felt waves of light and joy, just holding it and looking at it.

Charlotte noticed where the rock had sheared off from its mother rock, which was still embedded deeply in the earth. It was an ancient rock, surely, probably having been in this place for eons. How it floated up to be stumbled upon was a great curiosity to Charlotte. She sat down on the wooded hillside and held the rock, meditating.

An angel's voice came to her, telling her that this was Bob's Christmas gift to her. His undying love had made its way through the dimensions, following her through the woods, offering her the gift of this beautiful rock. The symbolism was profound. Shaped like a heart, this rock had split from its "mate," which still resided in the woods. For Charlotte, it represented the split between their worlds, yet gave the clear message that life does go on. Hers was continuing in this here-and-now, and Bob's was continuing in his here-and-now. Surely, she thought, love is the connection between the worlds.

She and Bob would often find such treasures in the woods—the odd-shaped stone, the distinctive piece of wood—and marvel over them for hours, talking and sharing. Together, hands reaching across time and space, they now had found another treasure, one of the eternal heart. For the first time in many months, Charlotte felt true joy.

The Christmas season was blessed for Charlotte with this personal gift from Bob. She brought the stone home as a constant reminder of the great heart of her beloved and the undying bond between them.

An Angel
and a Spare

$\mathcal{M}$ ardell had made up her mind: She and her two small sons were going home to her family for Christmas and for good. All she had to make the 2,000-mile journey was a broken-down truck with a bad transmission and $300 in savings. She didn't know how they would manage, but by the grace of God, she figured they would make the journey safely.

Just two months earlier, in October, Mardell's husband of one year had delivered a terrible shock: He was leaving her. Mardell had moved with her boys from Washington State to Dallas to be with him; now she felt abandoned. He told her he couldn't support her and the children because he was out of work. He gave her twenty dollars and an old, dilapidated truck and told her she could go stay at her uncle's home in Louisiana. Mardell couldn't see any other options, so she agreed.

The truck survived the trip from Dallas to Louisiana. Mardell's uncle and his wife took her and the boys in. The situation wasn't comfortable, but Mardell tried to make the best of it, pledging to herself that she would save every penny she could so that she and her sons could have their own home. Her goal was to go back to Washington, where her mother and stepfather lived.

She took three jobs. By the first week in December, she had saved $300. One night she came home late from her second job and found that her sons, Christopher, five, and C.C., seven, somehow had been locked out of the house and were sleeping in her uncle's old van. That was the last straw. She marched inside, collected their few belongings, and loaded up her ancient truck. They were going home to Washington then and there.

It was midnight when they set out on the road. The night was rainy and chilly. Inside, Mardell was terrified. She had never driven more than 100 or so miles in her life, let alone the 2,000 miles that stretched before her to Washington. She said a prayer with her sons, asking, *Please, God, get us home safe.* She alerted her mother, Joan, and stepfather, Chuck, that she was on her way. Joan and Chuck had no telephone; Mardell called a neighbor who lived not far from them in the eastern Washington countryside.

About an hour into the trip, Mardell suddenly realized that she didn't have a spare tire. What would she do if they had a flat? She prayed and prayed. Then there was the bad transmission. It whined and slipped, and Mardell wondered if it would give out at any moment, stranding them on some desolate stretch of road. All she could do was continue to pray, and hope that God and his angels would take care of them. If angels were real, this surely was the time for them to prove themselves.

Mardell headed west across Texas, New Mexico, and into Arizona. It was cold and the highways were icy, but mercifully no snow impeded their way. It was slow going in the old truck. "Come on, baby, come on, baby," she would coax.

At times terror would grip her and she literally shook. Little Christopher and C.C. would pipe up, "Don't cry, Mama!"

Mardell drove for long stretches, especially at night, pulling into rest areas during the day. They all slept in the truck, for she did not have enough money to pay for motels. They ate small breakfasts and lunches; she bought the boys one hot meal a day.

Once fatigue forced her to stop at night. Mardell pulled into an area she thought was a rest stop, and she and the boys slept. When dawn's light arrived, she was astonished to see that they were not at a rest stop, but at an isolated gravel pit. It gave her a shiver to think how vulnerable they'd been, had thieves been prowling the highway.

It took four days for the truck to wheeze to Nevada. Mardell held her breath repeatedly as the truck threatened to die. She checked the oil and transmission fluid once and was dismayed to find that both were very low—the oil was three quarts low. The tires were bald as well. At Hoover Dam, the truck labored up the steep road. On reaching the summit, smoke rolled from under the hood. Mardell discovered that the truck was out of oil and nearly out of water and transmission fluid. It took eight quarts of oil to return to running condition.

If worse comes to worst, I'll leave the truck and put us on a bus and get home that way, Mardell thought. Providing, of course, the truck broke down at a convenient location.

But the truck kept going, and Mardell began to feel that an angel certainly was with them, literally holding the truck together until they arrived at their destination.

Once a trucker in a large rig followed them, stopping at the same rest stops. At first Mardell was frightened, but the trucker proved to be an angel's agent. He approached her as she fed her boys cold cereal, and offered to buy them a hot meal. Mardell declined, but agreed to his offer to follow her as long as possible in order to ensure her safety. Her escort lasted about 300 miles.

Two days and several more difficult dams later, Mardell and the boys rolled into the driveway of Joan and Chuck's house in eastern Washington. What a relief! It was almost too good to be true. Mardell had made it with three dollars in her pocket to spare. And they'd had no flat tires, no transmission failures. Miraculously, the truck had gotten them home.

The next morning, Mardell got up and said she would go to the store for Joan. When she went out to her truck, she saw to her astonishment that it was sitting lopsided. One of the rear tires was completely flat. It could have happened anywhere along the 2,000-mile journey, out in the middle of nowhere in the middle of the night, or on a mountain pass.

Now Mardell knew without a doubt that she and her sons had been protected by an angel, who literally had been their spare until they reached home safe and sound.

A
Christmas Gift
from an
"Angel Animal" Cat

He was a kitten who would deliver a Christmas present as helpful and protective as the blessings a guardian angel might bestow. But on first encounter, no one could have predicted what a spiritually aware cat he would become.

Linda and Allen Anderson, creators and publishers of *Angel Animals® Newsletter,* found the kitten by answering a sign visible from the highway that they traveled to work each day in Minneapolis. It said, "Litter of Kittens—Free." Their beautiful golden retriever, who was best friends with their cat, Feisty, had died about six months earlier. Linda and Allen and Feisty grieved for the loss of her loving presence in their lives. But Feisty seemed to be drifting away from them also, sitting in the window hour after hour, awaiting his buddy's return. So they thought that perhaps adopting a kitten would help the whole family to heal.

When they went to the home where the kittens had been advertised, only one of them remained. He was a slender gray and brown tabby with green eyes that begged them to take him home. When Linda picked up the kitten, he clung to her and purred like a freight train. As loudly as a kitten can communicate, he shouted, "Get me out of here!"

The couple who were giving him away explained that their toddler had been confusing this kitty with a Ninja warrior and they'd found him trying to strangle the little fellow. These experiences had understandably turned the kitten into a bundle of nerves. Also, since he was the smallest of the litter, the other kittens ate all the food before he could wiggle his way to the bowl. The couple weren't sure if he'd ever really gotten enough to eat.

This was a kitten who definitely needed them, Linda and Allen agreed. And their family could use the healing energy of a kitten, even one who'd had such a rough start in life.

After they brought the kitten home, there were a few days of hissing by Feisty, but soon the older animal adopted him as a little brother and the two became the best of pals. But the kitten, unsure of the Andersons and himself, remained fearful. He would run away at the slightest provocation. They named him Speedy for the swiftness with which he could disappear when he felt the slightest bit threatened. They affectionately referred to Speedy as their resident scaredy-cat. He'd work up his nerve to inch close to them for an occasional petting but would run to hide under the bed if a strange sound or person appeared to threaten his security. Speedy would never stay in a room with anyone other than the Andersons.

When they'd had Speedy for several years, an unfortunate situation developed with one of their dearest friends. Misunderstandings resulted in this man, Steve (a pseudonym), deciding that he didn't want to visit Linda and Allen anymore or even talk on the telephone. It was a turn of events that made them feel very sad because Steve was someone they loved. Now a relationship they valued seemed to be lost forever.

Over the months, the Andersons often talked about Steve and wondered what, if anything, they could do to reestablish communication with him. They discussed what they had done to help create this situation. And they realized that although they felt hurt by Steve, they had also been insensitive to him. Linda and Allen vowed that if he ever gave them the chance to heal the wounds they all had inflicted on each other, they would do their best to make things right. With all their hearts, they hoped that someday the opportunity would come for the three of them to restore the bonds of friendship.

On Christmas Eve, it had been almost a year since Linda and Allen had last spoken with Steve. The Minnesota streets were covered with a glaze of snow, making it a picture-perfect holiday. Having Christmas Eve dinner with Steve had become a family tradition. Although they didn't talk about it, they both felt a little sad as they remembered him fondly and wished he were with them once again.

A knock at the door interrupted their meal preparations. Linda and Allen were surprised to find Steve standing on the doorstep with a Christmas card in his hand and a shy, uncertain look on his face. They invited him inside and greeted him warmly. He looked relieved. Immediately, they asked him to stay for dinner and he accepted.

During dinner, there seemed to be an unspoken agreement not to speak about the differences that had separated the three. Instead, they talked like old friends who had sincerely missed each other. They were very careful not to hit on any past-problem land mines. It was as if they'd all managed to jump aboard the same train taking them to a familiar destination.

But after dinner, everyone adjourned to the living room and the atmosphere chilled a little. The chitchat was over and now the painful past hung as heavily as a funeral pall over the conversation. Linda and Allen each realized that they needed help. What could they say? What shouldn't they mention? It was hard to know where to go next. They found themselves quietly praying for God's guidance in how to handle the situation.

As silently as an angel, Speedy tiptoed into the living room. Totally uncharacteristically for him, he moved toward Steve and gently rubbed his body against Steve's leg. Knowing what an unusual act it was for this cat, Steve gratefully scratched Speedy's head and let himself receive the love that seemed to pour from the little good will ambassador.

For the rest of the evening, Speedy stayed nearby and performed a most angelic function—he protected Linda, Allen, and Steve from hurting each other. This usually reticent cat acted as an emotional barometer to let everyone know how they were doing in the sensitivity department. If Linda or Allen said something that caused uneasiness in Steve, Speedy would back off and give them a look as if to say, *Better be careful with that.* When the conversation flowed easily, Speedy would purr and move closer to Steve, often licking his hand as if to reassure the Andersons that they were giving the right strokes to their friend.

As a result of Speedy's angelic intervention, all went well and the three made plans to get together again. After that evening Steve's friendship was restored and the Andersons were very happy to have him back in their lives again. But since that one Christmas Eve, when Linda and Allen needed him the most, Speedy has never joined them on subsequent visits with Steve (or anyone else), preferring to stay hidden from view until the guests leave.

On that special Christmas Eve, Speedy, so frightened and abused as a kitten, taught Linda and Allen a lesson in courage and sensitivity that they will never forget. Speedy is what they call an "angel animal," a messenger who lets people know that they are loved and that miracles are possible.

The
Greatest Gift

*J*t was a wrap on the movie destined to become one of the biggest moneymakers of film history: James Cameron's *Titanic.* For Joe Almazan, being part of the crew in the making of the movie was exciting. He loved working in the film industry. He had landed the job in purchasing with the help of his father's cousins, who worked in special effects. Jobs in the movie business are tough to get, and some who knew Joe would say, well, that's Joe's lucky stars again.

But on one October day, the stars unexpectedly dimmed.

Joe was on his lunch break when a friend stopped by for a chat. The young man seemed to need a sympathetic ear. Thoughtful and considerate, Joe was a good listener. The friend began to talk about his mother, who recently had been diagnosed with a tumor in her neck.

As Joe listened, he found himself unconsciously rubbing his own neck.

"Gosh, I'm really sorry to hear about that—it's sad," he told the friend. He kept rubbing his neck, and then stopped in astonishment. "You know, I feel a little lump on my neck as well."

The friend shook his head. "You better get that checked out. You never know—it could be cancerous."

Later, Joe telephoned his parents, Pat and Joe Senior, who lived about sixty miles away. Pat took the call. Joe relayed his odd story. She agreed that it would be wise to consult a doctor about the lump, but didn't think it was a serious matter. Joe was only twenty-nine years old, in the peak of vitality, despite childhood asthma. He had lots of energy that spilled out into an enthusiasm for life that made him popular with others. "Don't worry about it," she told Joe. "You're healthy."

Joe's doctor opined that the lump might be nothing more than a swollen lymph node. He gave Joe a prescription for antibiotics and told him to come back in two weeks.

Two weeks later, Joe was back in the doctor's office. The lump was still present in his neck. The doctor said, "Now I've got to biopsy it."

The results of the biopsy sent the entire Almazan family reeling in a state of shock. Joe was diagnosed with cancer: Hodgkins lymphoma stage II.

Pat especially could not comprehend where this malignant thing had come from, for Joe had no outward symptoms of being ill at all. Surely it was a mistake.

The family had to face learning a strange new language: the terminology of cancer and cancer care. Hodgkins lymphoma, they learned, is one of the most curable, especially if caught early. That was especially heartening. Stage II, they learned, meant that the cancer had already spread from its original site in Joe's neck. Lumps were on both sides of his neck, and a mass was growing in his chest behind his sternum. That wasn't so heartening. Still, the doctors were optimistic, estimating a 70 percent chance of recovery.

The family took the high road of optimism, too. Always close to one another, Pat, Joe Senior, Joe, his older sister, Cindy, and her husband, Steve, bonded even closer to support young Joe. So did Joe's sunny fiancée, Lisa. It wasn't just Joe who had cancer; the entire family shared in it as well. Everyone made the time to attend all of Joe's initial visits to the doctor, providing support that could not be measured in words.

Pat was grateful that the disease had been discovered before it had advanced into stage III or stage IV, when it becomes much harder to cure.

In stage III, the cancer spreads down to the stomach and other organs. In stage IV, it spreads throughout the body, and possibly into the bones. Joe's early discovery was no accident, of that she was certain.

"That was your angel speaking through your friend, telling you to get checked," she told Joe.

Joe agreed. Throughout his childhood years, Pat had told him about his angel guides, and that he had more than one. That it was important to listen to the inner voice to hear what his angels had to say to guide him. "You're right," he told his mom. "I never rub my neck like that. And if I hadn't done it just then, I would never have known until maybe it was too late."

Treatment had to begin right away. That meant postponing Joe's and Lisa's wedding, which had been planned for the following February.

Joe began his chemotherapy. Joe Senior, Pat, Cindy, and Lisa were with him at all treatments, feeling their presence was crucial to Joe's healing. The process was difficult and debilitating. Watching her youngest child endure the side effects with quiet courage tore Pat's heart. The stress exacerbated her own chronic condition of lupus, but she refused to let it get the better of her.

Joe maintained a strong outlook. "I'll get over this, I'll get through it," he kept reassuring Pat. "There's a reason for this. There's a reason for everything."

Two months into the chemotherapy, Joe's doctor said that he thought that Joe had better than a good chance to beat his cancer—in the high nineti-eth percentile. With Christmas nearing, this good news was the best present the family could receive. They were joyous! More than ever, the family felt closer together, and closer to the divine Spirit of Christmas.

Early in December, Pat began rummaging through her closets to bring out her boxes of cherished Christmas decorations. Every year, she lovingly unpacked the carefully wrapped ornaments and decorations, each of which was a treasury of memories. Why, she still had ornaments made by the child-ish hands of Joe and Cindy from their grade school days. She admired them just as much now as she did when they presented them to her years ago with shining faces. Just to look at the ornaments and hold them rekindled a fresh flood of warm feelings and happy memories.

But one ornament had long been missing from the collection. It was a lit-tle Santa Claus that young Joey had fashioned from cookie dough and painted. Though Pat was meticulous about wrapping and storing all the Christmas deco-rations in the same boxes at the end of every season, this little Santa had myste-riously vanished some seventeen years earlier. It just seemed to blip off into the ether. Over the years it had become the subject of occasional family jokes.

Pat had given up hope of finding it years ago. Now she picked her way through the boxes, unrolling reindeer, stars, colored globes, and glittery tree ornaments, thinking about Joe coming home for the holiday.

Suddenly Pat could not believe her eyes. Her breath caught and her skin prickled in goose bumps. There, nestled among the tree ornaments, was Joe's missing Santa, looking just as it had the last time she'd laid eyes on it.

The little Santa blurred as her eyes veiled with tears. For a moment, she simply could not believe it. Then her heart swelled with joy, and the tears turned to sobs. Pat cried and cried for what seemed like hours. Through it all, she felt a mysterious, radiant angelic presence—Joe's angel—that silently conveyed to her, *Everything will be all right.* Relief penetrated deep into her heart, into her bones.

When at last the sobs stopped, Pat gently took the precious Santa and hung him at the top of the tree. *Joe's going to pull through this,* she thought. *I know it.*

When Joe arrived for the family festivities, Pat waited until he admired the tree.

"Do you notice anything different?" she asked playfully.

Joe's eyes widened as he spied the long-missing ornament. "You found the Santa! Mom, where was it?"

Pat gave him an enormous grin. "You won't believe it. I found it right where it should have been, with the rest of the ornaments."

Joe shook his head, laughing. "I *don't* believe that."

"It was your angel," she said. "I thought the Santa was gone forever, but your angel found it and gave it back to us. It's a sign, Joe—a good sign that everything is going to be fine."

It was a happy but sober Christmas. The house filled with relatives and friends. Everyone was acutely aware of the joy of simply being together, sharing the time that now was so precious. Joe's little Santa glistened from the tree, a reminder that the greatest gift of all is life—and life that is filled with love.

After the chemotherapy, Joe underwent radiation, opting to handle these treatments on his own. Like other cancer patients, Joe felt his energy sapped by the side effects. An unexpected complication occurred when it was discovered that the radiation had burned Joe's asthma-sensitive lungs, damaging them. The condition could be medically treated, but nonetheless posed another hurdle.

A determined Joe kept his concentration on clearing the cancer from his system for good. He made steady progress. Planning went forward on his wedding for October. Tension eased; it appeared the angel's promise was at hand.

Then in May, the family was jolted by the prospect of devastating news. It appeared that the cancer mass in Joe's sternum was not responding well to the radiation therapy. Doctors voiced the possibility that the cancer might be more aggressive than originally thought. If tests revealed that to be the case, Joe would face more chemotherapy and perhaps stem cell replacement therapy.

Pat called more than ever on the power of prayer for Joe. She contacted everyone she knew and asked them to pray for him. She called prayer services. She requested Masses to be said for him. She had always believed in the healing power of prayer, and now she poured an intensity into that certainty, that faith. *We need you to work overtime on this,* she told Joe's angel.

She got down on her knees and prayed her rosary continually, prefacing each decade with *This is for Joe, that he be totally cured of cancer.* She also prayed for the family: *Please, dear God, give us the strength to get through this, whatever happens according to your will.*

For several weeks, the family held its breath, waiting for the outcome of a battery of tests. Pat could think of little else. Everything seemed to require a monumental effort. Time dragged by.

At last the results were in. The doctors were baffled. The tests showed no signs of cancer in Joe's body. What had appeared to be a lingering cancer tumor behind the sternum was judged to be only scar tissue. Joe was free—free of the killer that had invaded his body.

Praise God! exulted Pat. *This miracle happened because of all the prayers on Joe's behalf.*

His life now off hold, Joe began the process of recovery in earnest. Slowly, his lungs healed from the radiation burns.

Joe decided not to return to the film industry. In August, just ten months after his cancer was first detected, he entered a recertification program for training as a police officer. Many members of his family wore the badges of law enforcement and firefighters, including his father and his brother-in-law, Steve, both firefighters for Los Angeles County. Joe had worked briefly as a sheriff after his graduation from prestigious Pitzer College in Claremont, California. Law enforcement, he felt, was in his blood—his true soul's calling.

In October, a year after his fateful discovery of the lump, Joe and Lisa were married.

Pat remained committed more than ever to the power of prayer. Her daily rosary prayers were expanded to include many others who faced cancer, as well as other challenges.

The little Santa Claus ornament lies safely tucked away in its box between seasons. It has a most special meaning now. Brushed by an angel's hand, it—like Christmas itself—is a symbol of hope, renewal, and joy.

Resources

Angelhaven.com

For anyone interested in learning more about angels and sharing angel experiences, I highly recommend Angelhaven.com. This wonderful Website is the vision of Norm Braverman, of Bloomingburg, New York, who gives angel aficionados the world over a place to learn and chat. Thousands of visitors cross paths here every month. Here you'll find a chat room, prayer circle, frequently asked questions about angels, angel-related news, personal experiences, and an extensive selection of articles and columns. Join me in my corner for "Rosemary's View from the Rainbow Bridge," a regular inspirational column. You can share your own personal experiences, letters, and comments for others to read. There are angel-related business opportunities to explore.

What's more, Angelhaven.com goes beyond angels. By bringing people together to talk about love, compassion, forgiveness, faith, and all the fruits of the Spirit, it provides a source of spiritual nourishment we all need. The Web address is www.angelhaven.com.

The Compassionate Friends, Inc.

This nonprofit self-help organization is one of many for bereaved parents. The Compassionate Friends has chapters in every state. It provides a lifeline of support, friendship, and understanding to families who have lost a child of any age. Besides chapter meetings, it offers a quarterly magazine, book and audio tape resources, and regional and national events. The Website address is www.jjt.com/~tcf_national/, and gives contact information for local chapters. E-mail is tcf_national@prodigy.com. Or contact The Compassionate Friends at PO Box 3696, Oak Brook, IL 60522-3696.

Angel Animals® Newsletter

Allen and Linda Anderson are co-editors of the *Angel Animals® Newsletter*, a bimonthly, internationally distributed publication with inspiring stories from people all over the world who share how connecting spiritually with animals has made them healthier, wealthier, and wiser. They are the authors of *Angel Animals, Exploring Our Spiritual Connection with Animals,* published by Dutton-Signet. For a free sample of the *Angel Animals® Newsletter,* call 1-888-925-3309. Visit the Andersons' Website at www.angelanimals.com.

Silent Unity Prayer Service

For prayer support, I personally recommend Silent Unity, a twenty-four-hour-a-day nondenominational prayer service offered by the Unity School of Christianity, founded in the 1880s by Charles and Myrtle Fillmore. For more than a century, Silent Unity has served people of all faiths around the globe. Call for prayer support for any need at 1-816-969-2000. Or, write to Silent Unity at 1901 NW Blue Parkway, Unity Village, MO 64065.

About the Author

Rosemary Ellen Guiley is a renowned expert on spirituality, mystical and visionary experience, and the paranormal. She is a frequent and popular lecturer on such topics as angels, prayer, healing, dreams, spiritual awakenings, and mysteries of the unknown. She serves on the board of directors of the Association for the Study of Dreams. Among her previous books are *Wellness: Prayers for Comfort and Healing; Blessings: Prayers for the Home and Family; The Miracle of Prayer;* and *Angels of Mercy,* all published by Pocket Books. She lives with her husband near Annapolis, Maryland.